FROM EVERY NATION

FROM EVERY NATION

Derin Head Rodriguez

Deseret Book Company
Salt Lake City, Utah

© 1990 Derin Head Rodriguez

All rights reserved. No part of this book may be reproduced
in any form or by any means without permission in writing
from the publisher, Deseret Book Company, P.O. Box 30178,
Salt Lake City, Utah 84130.

Deseret Book is a registered trademark of Deseret Book Company.

Library of Congress Cataloging-in-Publication Data

Rodriguez, Derin Head.
    From every nation / by Derin Head Rodriguez.
      p. cm.
    Includes index.
    ISBN 0-87579-251-0
    1. Mormons—Biography.   I. Title.
BX8693.R63   1990
289.3'092'2—dc20
[B]   90-41043
                                            CIP

Printed in the United States of America

10   9   8   7   6   5   4   3   2   1

CONTENTS

PREFACE

"This is the beginning of an international church."

President Spencer W. Kimball was speaking to Elder Adney Y. Komatsu on the morning of April 3, 1975. He had just extended a calling to Elder Komatsu, a man born of Japanese ancestry and reared in the rigid customs and religion of that Far Eastern country, to serve as a General Authority of The Church of Jesus Christ of Latter-day Saints. Elder Komatsu's calling was the first of its kind to be extended to a non-Caucasian in this dispensation. With these simple words, President Kimball acknowledged that this calling was the symbolic beginning of a new era of growth and prophetic fulfillment for the Church.

The next morning, the prophet told an audience of millions in the opening session of general conference, "Truly this is now a world church. We are approaching the covering of the earth with the gospel as the depths are covered with the mighty oceans." (*Ensign*, May 1975, p. 5.)

Since that spring morning in 1975, many more General Authorities have been and continue to be called from lands far removed from Church headquarters in Salt Lake City — from Europe, Asia, Mexico, Australia, New Zealand, and Central and South America. Peoples in many other lands are also beginning to see the dawning of the gospel light rise on their borders, from the countries of Africa, the Middle and Far East, and Eastern Europe. I have been thrilled to be a latter-day witness of recent world events. Surely these happenings signal as never before the sign of the Lord's hand upon the earth, as he readies myriad and populous countries to receive the gospel. These are fertile fields for the Lord's harvest and may one day see not only hundreds of thousands of faithful converts but also valiant Church leaders and perhaps even General Authorities called from their midst.

This book contains biographies of fifteen General Authorities, all, except for Elder Komatsu, born and reared outside the United States. The individuals are from widely varying backgrounds and situations, but all are alike in their great strength and faith, as well as their tenderness and compassion. I believe that as you read this book, you will find elements you can identify and empathize with, and things that will move and inspire you as well. Most of these men were converts to the Church. Some accepted the gospel with eager, willing hearts; others only after much study and overcoming feelings of reluctance and hesitancy. There are stories of danger and adventure, of racial prejudice and bigotry, of material and spiritual hardship, of feelings of self-doubt and inadequacy, and of love and pain.

Preparing the materials for this book has been one of the rich experiences of my life. As I interviewed each man and researched his life, I would come away feeling "This is going to be the best chapter," only to decide "No, this will be my favorite," as I moved on to the next one. Elder Carlos H. Amado from Guatemala, in his first general conference talk after being sustained as a member of the Second Quorum of the Seventy, referred to himself and his colleagues as "ordinary men with extraordinary callings." I hope that both qualities come through in this book — a sense of the ordinary, for these are human beings, with difficulties, problems, and weaknesses; as well as a glimpse of the extraordinary, their devotion, faith, and strength.

My previous experience in interviewing had not prepared me for the candor, honesty, and vulnerability I encountered. I was disarmed by the warmth and openness with which I was often received, and delighted by the humor and levity I had not expected. As I have asked what circumstances brought these men to this point in their lives and then searched for answers, I have found a rich trove of meaning and understanding. I shall ever be grateful to them for their generosity of spirit and willingness to share their time as well as their past experiences, emotions, and spirituality.

I have tried whenever possible to use examples illustrating the worldwide nature of the Church and to give a glimpse of what it means to be a Latter-day Saint in various parts of the world. Elder Angel Abrea from Argentina, called in 1978 as a Seventy, said he spent a big part of his life viewing the Church from south to north, but since his calling he has had to get used to viewing the Church from north to south. Many of us have a view of the Church from only one perspective — ours. It is my hope that learning of others' experiences can give a glimpse of a different perspective — to see what the gospel means to Latter-day Saints in different parts of the world. Through that slightly enlarged vision, maybe we will be better able to discern what the gospel means to us.

I am grateful to my husband, Michael, and our five children — Kara, Adam, Daniel, Jonathan, and David — for their love and encouragement, as well as their acceptance of meals often hours late, other chores left undone, and my occasional absence and frequent preoccupation. They have cheerfully pitched in to take up the slack. Without their support, this project would have never been completed. I also appreciate the help, interest, hours of babysitting, and delighted amazement (or amusement?) that I would be writing a book that I have received from other family members and friends.

During this project I have received an undeniable spiritual witness that these men have indeed been called by the Lord to do his work. Though they are from many nations, they are the Lord's witnesses first and members of a certain race or culture second. I have an irrevocable testimony of their callings and of the gospel of Jesus Christ and the urgency of the task before all Latter-day Saints, to carry that message throughout the world.

A wise man once said, "When you write your history, take from the altars of the past the fire, not the ashes." If you receive even a portion of that same fire within these pages, this project will have fulfilled its purpose.

ADNEY Y. KOMATSU

President Spencer W. Kimball greeted the couple warmly, grasping their hands in turn with both of his, and invited them to sit in the chairs that had been pulled close to the big desk. He inquired about their flight from Hawaii to Salt Lake City and about their children. Then, without additional comment, he walked around his desk, sat down in the high-backed leather chair, and gazed directly into the eyes of the man sitting across from him. "The Lord has called you to be a General Authority in his church. Are you willing to accept the call?"

Adney Y. Komatsu, who had expected to be released from his calling as a regional representative, was speechless. His gaze fell to the floor while questions rapidly exploded like fireworks through his brain. *What is he saying? Did I hear right? Perhaps he made a mistake.*

1

After what seemed like an eternity but was probably only two or three minutes, President Kimball stood up and asked, "Are you all right? Do you want to go back to your hotel and pray about this?"

Finally Brother Komatsu raised his head and, in a whisper, asked, "President, you said the *Lord* called me?"

"That's right."

"Of course I accept. When I meet the Lord someday, how could I explain it if I refused his call?"

"Wonderful, wonderful!" President Kimball beamed, the tension in the room released by his wide smile. He sat down, leaned back in his chair, and said thoughtfully, "You are the first non-Caucasian to be called as a General Authority." Then, in measured tones, he added, "This is the beginning of an international church."

President Kimball's comment that morning in April 1975 was indeed historic. The next day in general conference he said, "Truly this is now a world church. . . . We are approaching the covering of the earth with the gospel as the depths are covered with the mighty oceans." (*Ensign*, May 1975, p. 5.) To meet the changing nature of a church spreading "to the four corners of the earth and to the ends of the world" (ibid., p. 4), General Authorities began to be called from lands far removed from Church headquarters in Salt Lake City — from Europe, Asia, Canada, Mexico, Australia, New Zealand, Central America, and South America.

"In a way, I guess I was the first," recalls Elder Komatsu today. "Although I was born an American, I was raised Japanese. I don't have blue eyes and blond hair — I have Oriental features and my parents were both from Japan. That made me different from those who had previously been called as General Authorities."

Elder Komatsu is used to being a first. He was the first member of his family to join the Church, the first Latter-day

Saint bishop of Japanese descent, the first Japanese mission president, as well as the first Japanese regional representative. Although he takes the responsibilities of his positions very seriously, whenever he speaks of himself there is always a good deal of his characteristic, self-deprecating humor mixed in. "I feel like Jackie Robinson when he broke the color line in baseball's major leagues," he confesses. "I just tell myself that I've got to be careful not to do anything that will keep them from calling other Japanese people because of something I did."

That April of 1975, Elder Komatsu was sustained as an Assistant to the Council of the Twelve. Six months later the First Quorum of the Seventy was established, and in October 1976 he became a member of that body. He has found his calling as a General Authority to be uniquely challenging. "It is easy to say you accept the call, but once you get involved in it you find it is one of the most challenging jobs there is," he says. "My calling was devastating to me because I felt I was not prepared for it. I had not been raised in the Church, and, although I'd had many years of service as a bishop, a mission president, and so forth, I had never been what you would call a scholar of the scriptures."

Because his parents never became members of the Church, Elder Komatsu is keenly cognizant of the rich heritage shared by many who are fourth-, fifth-, or even sixth-generation Latter-day Saints. "You'd better appreciate your illustrious background, the ancestors who struggled, sacrificed, and even died so that you could be here today," he often tells members of the Church at conferences in stakes populated by multigenerational Latter-day Saints. Then he cautions, "See to it that you set your own houses in order so that your children and your children's children will be born in the covenant, go on missions, marry in the temple, and carry on the work of the Lord."

"I am the first generation in the House of Komatsu to be a member of the Church," he explains. "My wife and I have four children, who are second-generation members, and four grandchildren, who are the third generation of Latter-day Saints in the House of Komatsu. If I live perhaps twenty years longer, I will be in my late eighties and my grandchildren will be asking me, 'Grandpa, will you marry us in the temple?' and I hope I will be able to do so. In any event, if they have children, the fourth-generation Mormons will finally be born in the House of Komatsu — four generations of covenant children. To me, that is the greatest accomplishment I could have made during my time here on this earth. Knowing that your children, grandchildren, and great-grandchildren are continuing to live the gospel is more soul satisfying than any position or honor you can achieve in the world."

Elder Komatsu's concern about his posterity is mirrored by his interest in his predecessors. Because he was raised in a culture that reveres one's ancestors and has also taken to heart the Church's emphasis on genealogy, Elder Komatsu is doubly determined to research his roots and complete the temple work for his deceased relatives. Although this has been especially difficult because both of his parents are from Hiroshima, Japan, where many records were destroyed in an atomic bombing near the end of World War II, he has been able to complete family group sheets extending back several generations. "When I go over to the other side and meet my God and all of my ancestors, I want to be able to say that I have fulfilled my responsibilities to the House of Komatsu," he says.

This heightened awareness of familial ties and obligations was planted in young Adney by his parents, Jizaemon and Misao Tabata Komatsu. Misao was seventeen years old and living in Japan when she became a "picture bride." Following an established Japanese custom, she was shown a picture of

Jizaemon Komatsu by his parents and told, "This is our son who has moved to Hawaii. Will you be willing to travel there and marry him?" Because the name Komatsu was an honorable and revered one, she agreed.

When she arrived in Hawaii, her heart sank as she discovered that her prospective husband was not anywhere near the age of twenty-one, which had been represented to her. In fact, he was thirty-seven—though to her he seemed much older than that—and had been married twice before. However, being an obedient young woman, Misao honored her family's commitment and the marriage took place as planned. The couple eventually had five children; Adney Yoshio was the second, born August 2, 1923.

Family life in the 1920s and '30s was not easy for the Komatsus, who were desperately poor. Although both parents worked long hours in a pineapple cannery, their small depression-era paychecks didn't stretch very far. Despite their hard work, the family was often forced to rely on welfare merely to stay alive. Yet no matter how meager their food supplies, the first and choicest bits from their table were always offered to the Shinto shrine on the kitchen wall. Like most Japanese families, the Komatsus affiliated with both the Shinto and the Buddhist traditions. They found the emperor-worship aspects of Shintoism and the after-life implications of Buddhism compatible and essential in adding faith, structure, and order to their lives.

Jizaemon, plagued with gallstones and stomach problems most of his adult life, was often hospitalized for weeks at a time and died at the age of forty-nine, when Adney was eleven years old. Today Elder Komatsu's memories of his father are few and faded, although vivid in his mind are images of the day his father was brought home from the hospital so that he might die with his family close by. The children, ages two to thirteen, had been unable to visit their father in the hospital,

5

and now, the sight of the dying man stretched out Japanese-style on a quilt in the middle of the living room floor upset them, as they struggled to understand what was happening. Though the family had no relatives in Hawaii, many friends and neighbors gathered to keep a vigil with the grieving wife. Just before he died, Jizaemon pulled Misao close to him and, in a raspy whisper, instructed her to continue to raise their children in the Buddhist faith. She vowed to do so.

After his death, existence became even more of a struggle for his widow and five children. To help make ends meet, Misao would bring home laundry, which the children would scrub, starch, and iron while she was at work. "They were oil-soaked garagemen's clothes that were almost impossible to clean," remembers Elder Komatsu. "We children would boil them in a large pan on the stove and then scrub them with a bar of harsh soap to get the grease out. It was a rough life for the young ones."

Adney also began working evenings, selling popcorn and peanuts in a local theater; on a good night he would make twenty-five or thirty cents in commissions. Misao would stop by to walk home with her son, and when he had done well she would ask him, "Would you like to stop for a nickel bowl of noodles? You've earned it tonight." The five cents, of course, came out of his earnings, which he dutifully turned over to his mother.

It was far from an idyllic childhood, and the Komatsu children grew up knowing hunger, poverty, and hard work. In the rigid atmosphere of their home, they developed an adherence to strict rules and rigorous expectations, receiving in return few displays of parental affection. "The Japanese approach to child rearing is more hands off, not hugging and kissing their children the way people of many other cultures do," says Elder Komatsu. As a result, he admits to having been a stern father with his own family, though his children tend to view him in a softer light. He is "dutiful, responsible, serious," and at the same time "a kind and gentle person—a fine example of a loving father," according to one son. Elder Komatsu concedes that the years have softened his approach and mellowed the gruffness in his manner. "My grandchildren climb all over me like I am a horse," he adds with a wry grin.

When Adney was fifteen years old, his thirteen-year-old brother came home after playing football and complained of a headache. He went to bed and didn't get up even to eat. Two days later he was dead. The family was understandably shaken. While they never knew the definite cause of his death (they suspected a head injury from a rough football tackle), Misao was overwhelmed with grief and guilt, feeling that because she had been so busy working, she hadn't given her son the time or attention he needed. Perhaps if she had, she thought, things might have turned out differently.

About that same time, Adney, taller than most of his peers, was asked by two Mormon missionaries to join a Church-sponsored basketball team. He was so awkward and lanky that he despaired of ever making a good ball player, but the elders took a special interest in him. He was soon attending meetings of the Young Men's Mutual Improvement Association regularly, and the missionaries began pressuring him to go to Sunday School. When he finally did, he liked it so much he also began attending sacrament meeting, and for a whole year he never missed a meeting.

After spending several months reading the Joseph Smith story and studying the gospel with the missionaries, Adney had the beginnings of a firm testimony and turned the tables on the elders, asking them if he could be baptized. They agreed, but with one stipulation: he needed his mother's permission.

He was seventeen years old and a high school graduate

7

when he approached his mother and asked her to allow him to join The Church of Jesus Christ of Latter-day Saints. She immediately started crying, and he asked, "Are those happy tears?"

"Tears of sadness," she said.

"But why? I am going to church. That is something a good boy does. Besides, you work all day long, and I need some activity to be involved in."

"But I promised your father I would raise you in the Buddhist faith. I lost one son because I was too busy, and now, because I haven't paid you enough attention, I am about to lose another son."

"Mother, you won't be losing a son—you will be gaining a better one," he responded. "In the year that I have been associating with the missionaries, I have found a purity and a cleanliness that I haven't found anywhere else. There is something about them that builds me up."

He then offered to make a deal with her: "If you will permit me to join the Mormon church, I will live the best life that I can. But if you find that I cause you any trouble or embarrassment, if I commit any shameful or dishonorable act, then all you have to do is ask me to quit going to church and I will obey, without question. But on the other hand," he continued, "if I become a better person, more kind and attentive to your needs and those of my brothers and sister, then would you give me your blessing? Because I know that this church is the place I can gain an education for an eternal life."

She agreed to the bargain, and the day never came when she asked her son to leave the Church. She died a few years later of a brain hemorrhage, caused by high blood pressure, at the age of forty-nine, the same age at which her husband died. If Adney was anguished by his father's passing, his mother's death left him devastated. At her funeral, his bishop was the single Caucasian in a long line of Japanese mourners, a fact that brought tears to his eyes. "Here was a bishop who really cared about me," he said. "He didn't know my mother, but he honored her and he honored me by his presence."

Neither Jizaemon nor Misao Komatsu, nor any of their children other than Adney, ever joined the Church. However, Elder Komatsu has had the temple work done for his parents and deceased brothers and anticipates the time when his family will be sealed together.

Soon after his baptism in 1941, Adney was called to be the Sunday School superintendent. However, the manual said that the superintendent was supposed to have meetings in his home, and because his mother and brother both smoked, he felt that the atmosphere would not be conducive to the Spirit of the Lord. He declined the calling, the first and only time he ever turned down a calling from the Lord, and as his spirituality matured, he would serve in a wide range of leadership positions.

Through his teens, the promise he had made to his mother was always uppermost in his mind and gave him added incentive to live gospel principles. During World War II Adney served in the U.S. Army's 441st Counterintelligence Corps. At the close of the war he had the opportunity to visit Japan as a member of the U.S. Army of Occupation, the first of many visits to the land of his heritage.

Returning to Hawaii after his discharge, Adney began a career in business and finance. He was in his mid-twenties when he met Judy Nobue Fujitani, a beautiful young Japanese woman who was selling tickets at a community function. Adney had been assigned to protect her and keep the money safe, an assignment that he found highly pleasant.

"I must admit, I was impressed with him," Sister Komatsu said years later. "He was different from most men I knew. He didn't smoke or drink, and I had never met a fellow who was so honest and considerate." (*Church News*, May 3, 1975, p. 7.)

The attraction was mutual, and right away he asked her out — to church, of course. Soon they were dating frequently. Adney knew that what attracted Judy to him — his high standards of behavior and obedience to the Word of Wisdom — were qualities common to other Mormons as well, so, warily, he took her to church. He wanted her to have the opportunity to meet other priesthood holders and see if she would be attracted to any of them, though he made sure she kept enough distance so that couldn't happen.

Adney knew he wanted to marry a member of the Church, and so as their relationship progressed and they fell in love, he told her, "You have one foot in the Church already because you believe the principles. All you need to do is bring the other foot in and be baptized." Judy was getting some pressure at home, similar to what Adney had experienced when he became involved with the Mormons. Her mother, like Misao Komatsu, was a widow and a devout Buddhist who didn't like her daughter's Christian boyfriend or the idea that her daughter might not carry on the family's religious traditions after she was dead.

Although there were many tears, Judy's mother was present when Judy was baptized by Adney in 1948. But she was not able to attend at the couple's wedding in the Hawaii Temple on Friday, June 2, 1950, and there were many more tears. Mrs. Fujitani found very little comfort in the fact that none of the bridegroom's family was able to attend the ceremony either. Reversing the tradition of a wedding reception given in honor of the couple by the parents, on Saturday the newlyweds hosted a celebration for their families. They hoped it would bring both sides closer together and make them feel a part of their wedding. It did help to soothe some troubled feelings.

On the day after the reception, the couple attended church together in Judy's branch for the first time. (After Judy's baptism, Adney had felt it would be better if she went to meetings on her own so she could develop a testimony without influence or pressure from him. They would each go to Sunday School in their own branch in the morning and then attend sacrament meeting together in Adney's branch later that day.)

Sacrament meeting had already started when they slipped into Judy's branch and sat in the back of the room, hoping to be relatively unnoticed. They were somewhat surprised to see the mission president conduct the meeting and release the branch presidency. But that was nothing compared to their surprise as the name Adney Y. Komatsu was presented for the sustaining vote of the congregation as the new president of the branch! In a state of shock, the twenty-seven-year-old president left his bride in the audience and walked up to the podium. The next day, which was supposed to be the first day of their honeymoon, he held a meeting in their apartment with his new counselors — with no complaints from Sister Komatsu.

That experience was just a sample of what lay ahead for the Komatsus, who have continuously served in leadership capacities ever since. When President Komatsu was called as a bishop eleven years later, President Hugh B. Brown asked if his wife would sustain him, knowing there would be no time to talk to her before the meeting. "You don't have to worry about that," Brother Komatsu assured him.

And he was right, for he has always been able to count on the total support of his wife, just as she has been able to rely on his support in her responsibilities and callings — and they have both been assured of a sustaining vote from their four children. The Komatsu family has always willingly relocated wherever the Lord has had a mission for them, although at times the changes in countries, cultures, and languages have proved demanding. The first move was from Hawaii to Japan in 1965, when Elder Komatsu was called as president of the Northern Far East Mission. There the whole family learned to speak Japanese and became acquainted firsthand with the country of their heritage.

In 1968 they returned to Hawaii, and two years later he was called as a regional representative over Japan and Hawaii. This assignment allowed him to live and work in Hawaii but also required frequent travel to Japan. During this time he was also a sealer in the Hawaii Temple and Sister Komatsu served as a temple worker for Japanese language sessions.

Elder Komatsu was the senior vice president and manager of the mortgage division of Honolulu Federal Savings and Loan Association, a firm he had been with for twenty-one years, and had just built a new home in Hawaii when he was called as a General Authority in 1975. He was one of the first six resident General Authorities, a new program in which each of these brethren would live in their area of responsibility. The Komatsus sold their new home and moved to Tokyo, where they would live for three years. Elder Komatsu spent one year as the executive administrator of the entire Asian area and, when the area was divided the next year, two years as administrator of the Church in Japan and Korea. In 1978 he went back to Hawaii with an assignment as executive administrator for the Pacific islands, including Hawaii, Micronesia, Fiji, Tahiti, and Tonga, and four and a half years later he was called back to Japan as president of the Tokyo Temple. In 1985 he moved to Salt Lake City to serve as second counselor in the Utah South Area presidency and as a counselor in the Sunday School general presidency. And in 1987, the Komatsus returned to the Orient, this time to Hong Kong, when Elder Komatsu became the first counselor in the area presidency.

Elder Komatsu's callings have often been callings for Sister

Komatsu as well. She served alongside him when he was a mission president, and as temple matron when he was president of the Tokyo Temple. In 1971, while he was serving as a regional representative, she was called as a member of the Relief Society general board, the first board member of Oriental descent, under Relief Society President Belle S. Spafford. In this position she had to travel frequently from Hawaii to the Orient and to Utah. She was released from this assignment in 1975 when Elder Komatsu was called as a General Authority. As the wife of a member of an area presidency, she has served as a representative of the general boards of the Relief Society, Young Women, and Primary in his assigned area. "Every weekend when I have a stake conference, she goes and teaches the auxiliary leaders, whether it be in Korean, Chinese, or Japanese," her husband explains.

One of Elder Komatsu's choicest experiences as a General Authority came at the close of a week spent in Salt Lake City for general conference, not long after he was sustained as a Seventy. At about 5:30 P.M. one day, as he was in his temporary office at the Church Office Building, preparing to return to the Far East, he decided to see if President Kimball was still in his office; he wanted to just drop by and tell him goodbye. Though the prophet was usually gone by that hour, President Kimball's secretary reported that he was still in and would be happy to see Elder Komatsu. Elder Komatsu later recalled that President Kimball rose and came across the office to greet him, affectionately clasping his hand in both of his own, and eagerly "shook my arm like he was trying to pump water from a dry well."

"I just came to tell you what a great conference it was and to thank you for your words. I'll see you in six months," Elder Komatsu said.

"Oh no, you're not going to get away that quickly!" President Kimball exclaimed. "Come over here and let's visit for a while." The two men sat side-by-side, President Kimball still holding his visitor's hand with both of his, and talked for about thirty minutes. Elder Komatsu responded to the prophet's questions about his childhood, family, and background and finally made a gesture to stand up, protesting, "President, I have taken too much of your time."

President Kimball reached over to give him a kiss on the cheek, but the younger man stood up quickly and the kiss fell on his lapel. Taken a bit off guard, President Kimball asked, "You Japanese don't kiss, do you?" still holding the younger man's hand.

"President, we don't show our emotions, but we love you just the same," he responded, looking down into the beloved face of a prophet of the Lord.

Elder Komatsu related later, "He grabbed me again with a bear hug like I have never been hugged in my life and gave me a big kiss right on the cheek. After that kiss he didn't let go, he just held me. Then he pulled my head down and whispered in my ear, 'Young man, I love you very much.' Well, by now I felt as if I were starting to rise off the floor. When you receive that kind of treatment from a prophet of the Lord, well . . . " Elder Komatsu's voice faltered and he shook his head. "I just held onto him and he held onto me and finally he said, 'The Lord loves you also.'

"Just imagine," said Elder Komatsu, childlike wonder echoing in his tone, "here's a living prophet telling me he knows who I am and that he loves me. And that the Lord, whom he represents, also loves me. I'll never forget that experience. I walked about a foot off the ground all the way back to my hotel."

Besides his honesty and candor, one of the qualities most loved in Elder Komatsu by those who associate with him, as well as the countless Latter-day Saints who hear him speak, is his lively sense of humor. His good-natured kidding is most often directed at himself, and usually has something to do with his Hawaiian and Japanese background.

"I am glad to see so many here," he began his talk at a recent stake conference where the rain was pouring down outside. "When it rains like this in Hawaii, everyone usually stays home. Of course," he said, smiling, "when it is sunny, no one comes either—they all go to the beach. That's why a Hawaiian always carries his swimming suit in here," he slips his hand in his back pocket—"he never knows when he'll have a chance to go swimming." In true island style, Elder Komatsu loves both swimming and surfing, though he gets few chances to do either these days. He is looking forward to his eventual retirement, when he and Sister Komatsu plan to move back to Hawaii. (In the October 1989 general conference it was announced that members of the First Quorum of the Seventy would be granted emeritus status at age seventy.)

Being an American of Japanese descent is another source for Elder Komatsu's humor. "Aloha," he will tell a congregation. "My name is Komatsu and I look Oriental, but I was born and raised in Hawaii. There is a real Japanese General Authority named Yoshihiko Kikuchi from Tokyo. I can tell you about King Kamehameha and the Hawaiian royalties, but if you have any questions about Japan, ask Elder Kikuchi, he's the real thing." He admits he is frequently mistaken for Elder Kikuchi, but he takes it all lightly, refusing to be bothered by the mistaken identity. Shrugging his shoulders, he quips, "Why not? All of you Caucasians look alike to us, too."

Though Elder Komatsu looks Oriental, there is no question that he is Hawaiian through and through, and is eager to move back to the "Garden of Eden," as he calls it. "This place is the lone and dreary world," he adds, his gestures making it clear that he includes every land mass but Hawaii in that category.

15

Invariably after he has spoken in a general or stake conference session, someone will come up and ask, "Where did you learn to speak English so well?" Without missing a beat he lapses into a heavy Japanese accent, a twinkle in his eye, and says, "Oh, I studdy velly hawd."

Adney Y. Komatsu has the ability to laugh at himself and enjoy life without allowing such levity to detract from his serious commitment to the gospel and his responsibilities. In fact, these qualities may be precisely what have kept him afloat in his arduous voyage from a young poverty-stricken Buddhist boy in Hawaii to an esteemed, beloved church leader. Any blessings and gifts of the spirit he has been given along the way, he has turned outward and used to bless the lives of others.

CHARLES A. DIDIER

Since he became a member of the First Quorum of the Seventy in October 1975, Elder Charles A. Didier has had the opportunity to touch the lives of millions of people all over the world through televised general conference talks and messages given in stake, mission, and regional conferences. But it is not this widespread influence that gives him the greatest feelings of joy and satisfaction in the service of the Lord. Rather, he counts as his choicest experiences his opportunities to meet with, counsel, and bless individual members of the Church on a person-to-person level.

"Often when I speak at a stake or regional conference, I leave without seeing any results of my time there and I wonder if I've been effective. I ask myself, 'Am I doing any good? Have I made any difference?' It can be such anonymous work at this level," he admits. "But it's different when you work one-on-one with people and have an opportunity to use your priesthood authority in counseling and uplifting others." That's why whenever he visits conferences, Elder Didier asks the local leaders to set up appointments beforehand with those who may wish to talk to him—

Like a sixty-year-old man in Arizona who had been confined to a wheelchair most of his life. Elder Didier visited the man in his simple, unpretentious home and learned that one of his most cherished dreams had always been to fill a mission. Elder Didier laid his hands on the man's head and promised him that not only would he walk again, but he would also realize his heart's delight in service to the Lord. Recently Elder Didier received a letter from the man, who enthusiastically recounted his experiences on a mission in Mexico.

And a couple in Texas who were filled with frustration and despair because they had not been able to have children and had already visited countless specialists and submitted to an endless array of tests and procedures. Elder Didier blessed the couple and told them not to worry, promising them that everything would be all right. A year later they sent him a picture of their new baby.

And a mother who recently called Elder Didier and told him, "You made a difference in my child's life." Her son had been sent home from the Missionary Training Center in Provo, Utah, a few years earlier because of unresolved problems. Elder Didier had counseled with him and, sensing the elder's repentant heart and strong desire to serve the Lord, had been able to help him put his life in order. "We just picked him up from his mission, and he is a changed person— a wonderful, strong young man," said the mother, her voice trembling with emotion. "You made him believe in the worth of his soul and in the work of the Lord. Thank you, thank you."

"It is in personal interaction that you feel you can accom-

18

plish things," says Elder Didier, emotion quivering in his voice. "It is the individual acts of love and charity that you remember, not the stake conferences."

These loving deeds have balanced the scales in Elder Didier's own life, because he credits his membership in the Church, as well as his calling as a servant of the Lord, to a great many individual acts of love and charity by others toward him. In general conference after having just been sustained as a Seventy, he declared, "If I am here today, I owe it to hundreds of hands which pushed me, pulled me, helped me, sustained me to be here today, in fact, to be a member of The Church of Jesus Christ of Latter-day Saints." (*Ensign*, November 1975, p. 57.)

Without the righteous influence of many key persons in his life, the young Belgian probably would not have found the path that was to lead him to become the first resident General Authority from Europe called in this dispensation. The journey began when he was born on October 5, 1935, in the Brussels suburb of Ixelles, Belgium, the eldest of four children born to André and Gabrielle Colpaert Didier. Charles grew up speaking French and Dutch, and later learned English, German, Spanish, and Portuguese as well. Living when and where he did, with his father a career officer in the Belgian army, it was inevitable that his life would be profoundly affected by World War II.

In 1940 the Germans invaded Belgium—as well as the secure, naive world of five-year-old Charles. Neither would ever be the same again. The Didiers were living in Vilvorde, another Brussels suburb, when he first saw armed troops marching down the street in front of their third-floor apartment. Shortly after the German occupation began, his father was taken prisoner in the first sweep of arrests of army officers. He was to be sent to Germany, but within three weeks he had escaped and immediately began working as a radio operator in the underground, communicating with the London Intelligence Service. For the next several months confusion reigned—the Germans were unorganized at the beginning of the occupation and didn't have a record of the prisoners' names, so they didn't know whom they were looking for—so André Didier was able to live at home with his family. But as he became increasingly involved with the resistance, the Gestapo stepped up efforts to find him and he fled, spending the rest of the war hiding from the Gestapo and working with the underground.

Except for his father's absence, Charles's life under German occupation was not much different than before. His mother, a resourceful, caring woman, instilled in her children a deep sense of love and security. War became a game to Charles and his peers, the soldiers marching in the streets not much different from their toy soldiers, somehow transformed into larger, animated replicas. This inability to sense the realities of war became a danger in itself as the children rushed out to watch the bombers flying overhead and collect the fallen shrapnel as souvenirs.

"I remember when enemy planes started day bombing in the city," Elder Didier recounts. "In order to confuse the radar, the planes would release aluminum strips, which would form big clouds on the radar screens. It was extraordinary to see—the sky filled with the glittering mass falling down around us."

When the bombing raids came at night, the family fled to the basement, where they crouched in the dark with friends and neighbors, their noses and mouths covered by white surgical masks to screen out the heavy dust from crumbling houses and other buildings. Only fifteen kilometers from the city's industrial center, Charles watched out the window as the city burned, vivid images of orange-red flames in the skyline indelibly blazed into his young consciousness. "I remember watching others hunched and trembling, but I thought how funny they looked with the masks on. I don't remember being afraid once during all of those experiences. I guess that was a blessing," he adds.

Gabrielle Didier struggled to protect and provide for her young children in her husband's absence. She worked in her home as a seamstress, with two other women coming every day to work with her. War and separation brings problems to a family, and Gabrielle and André, not able to be together to iron out their difficulties, solved them by being apart.

"My father was not a great, faithful family man," Elder Didier admits. "Mother was the one who held us together. She was a stalwart, dedicated, loving woman. We got our real education — our education in character, moral principles, honesty, and hard work — from her example. She knew her responsibility and acted accordingly. She was the captain."

Though his parents were baptized Catholics and his mother was a believer, the family didn't attend church and the children were never taught to pray. Because a religious home life had never existed, they didn't miss it. Instead Charles received a smattering of religious education at school, where for one hour a week he had his choice of studying Catholicism, Judaism (except during the war), or morals, which was a combination of the basic principles of morality, justice, and human behavior. He chose the latter.

Toward the end of the war, as food and other supplies became extremely scarce, school also became the source of minimal basic nutrition. Every day each student would get a dose of cod liver oil or a spoonful of tuna fish. On one special day in December 1943 each child received a Christmas gift — a shiny, fragrant orange donated by the Red Cross. Charles couldn't wait to take the wondrous item home, where it was reverently quartered and shared with other family members.

In 1944 the Gestapo, unable to locate André, came after

21

his family, and Gabrielle fled with her children to her parents' home in Brussels. They were reunited briefly with André in a forest in Flanders, and finally they traveled to her grand- mother's home in Audenaerde. This clandestine running and hiding on buses, trains, and streetcars was an adventure, a continuation of the game called war, for Charles, then nine years old.

On September 2, 1944, Allied troops came to Audenaerde, and for Charles—and at least for that part of Belgium—the war was over. The whole town turned out to cheer the lib- erating army as tanks rolled into town, flanked by the com- panies of soldiers. But the celebration quickly darkened into tragedy when a sudden explosion directly behind the Didiers rocked the area. The battle-wary townspeople instinctively hit the ground, and smoke and debris filled the air. Citizens and soldiers alike began screaming and running, some tug- ging on the bodies of the dead and maimed. A blood-spattered man, carrying a small child whose leg had been blown away, ran past Charles. Gabrielle, shifting her six-month-old baby on her hip, seized the hands of her two older children and they all bolted for shelter.

"People all around us were either wounded or killed. We were protected, but I don't know how," recalls Elder Didier. To this day the source of the explosion is unknown. "At that moment of liberation there was such confusion—troops en- tering the city on one side and just in front of them the Germans fleeing or hiding. And at the same time many of the local residents, I'm sorry to say, were stealing and looting, trying to get at the supplies that the Germans in their haste had left behind. Perhaps the explosion was caused by a mine, or maybe some remaining German troops wanted to leave something to be remembered by."

After the war the family returned to Brussels, where they lived until André, who was in northern Belgium and not liberated until much later, came home. Peacetime marked a new beginning for the Didiers, who were together as a family for the first time in many years. André reenlisted in the Belgian army and in 1947 was transferred to Namur as an engineer. There they rented a home — their first ever — and planted a garden, and their fourth child was born.

However, this seemingly idyllic life didn't last long. In 1950 André requested a transfer to Germany. Charles, now fifteen, was preparing to enter a military academy, and having a father in foreign service would give him an advantage in being accepted. But that wasn't the only reason for the transfer. André would be home only about three or four days a month, and the Didiers were again solving their problems by separation. But despite his father's foreign service, Charles wasn't accepted into the academy, and he entered the University of Liege to begin studying economics.

One hot summer day in 1951, the Didiers noticed two young American men bicycling up the hill toward their home. When the visitors knocked on their door, the family invited them in, out of curiosity if nothing more. They offered them something to drink and thought it strange that they preferred water to iced tea. Then everyone gathered around to hear their stories about American Indians and plates of gold. The missionaries had only their copies of the Book of Mormon and a few homemade visual aids — drawings and a book whose pages had been painted gold. Nevertheless they found an eager student in Gabrielle.

"My father was still in Germany and my mother was really looking for something to fill the void in her life," Elder Didier explains. "The missionaries' coming to our door was literally an answer to her prayers."

It was not long before Gabrielle was convinced that the message the young men brought was true, and she accepted their challenge to be baptized. But there was one problem:

they couldn't baptize her without her husband's permission. "She waited until he came home on leave," Elder Didier explains, "and then invited the missionaries over. One of them, Elder Smith, went for a walk with my father, and when they came back the elder was smiling." André had given his permission only on condition that the children would not be baptized until the age of twenty-one, which was fine with Charles, who didn't particularly want to be baptized.

So Gabrielle joined the Church and the missionaries became regular visitors at the Didier home, helping Charles with his English lessons, eating, and playing Monopoly and football. "We were great friends," according to Elder Didier. "It was almost like having a couple of big brothers. My mother wanted us to go to church with her. She was strong-willed and we were used to doing what she said, so we went."

Charles gradually became acquainted with the gospel doctrines, the missionaries, and the members of the twelve-member branch in Namur, but he was slow to gain a firm testimony. He had no problems with basic church doctrine, the life-style appealed to him, and he had never smoked or drunk. Also, painfully aware of the problems in his parents' relationship, he was attracted by the principle of eternal marriage. But something was missing.

Seeking counsel from his father, Charles was told, "The church is good, but its members are a minority in Belgium. [There were only 150 members in the entire district.] You will be a nobody here. And where are you ever going to find a wife who will accept your religion? Never, never marry someone who has a different religion."

"He was right in some of his counsel," says Elder Didier. "My mother wanted me to join the Church, but she never pushed me. She just told me to pray about it and make my own decision. So I did pray about it, and gradually that missing element, a solid testimony of the Book of Mormon, fell into place. Once it came, the rest was easy."

In November 1957, at age twenty-two, Charles Didier was baptized in a swimming pool in Brussels and became a member of The Church of Jesus Christ of Latter-day Saints. His two brothers and sister also joined the Church, but his father never did. A few years later his parents were divorced.

As a university student at Liege, Charles settled into membership in the Church, studying its history, learning about its programs, and becoming involved in its activities. As he became experienced in conducting meetings and giving talks, his shyness disappeared. His school work improved and he scored higher on his oral examinations.

At an activity of the Mutual Improvement Association he met a pretty young brunette, Lucie Lodomez, an aspiring opera singer. She had been a member of the small Liege Branch since she was fifteen years old. Since she lived near Charles's apartment, they would often walk home from MIA together, and they became friends, but no more than that. "I wasn't looking for anything more serious," he claims, adding, "and I wasn't very interested in opera . . . at the time."

Lucie was called to serve a mission in Paris, where she became a missionary companion to Charles's sister. In the meantime, Charles graduated from the university with the equivalent of a master of business administration and then entered the army. Several months later he received a letter from his sister inviting him to a youth conference in Switzerland, offering a rare opportunity for young Latter-day Saints from France, Belgium, and Switzerland to get together. Charles was granted a three-day pass, only to receive a telegram from his sister saying the conference dates had been changed. He was disappointed but unable to change his leave. But before he threw the pass away, he received a third message: the conference was back on.

He hitchhiked seven hundred miles to the conference and spent the three days there becoming reacquainted with his sister, but especially with Sister Lodomez. A dance was scheduled for the last day of the conference, which also happened to be the last day of Lucie's mission. The mission president, aware that something interesting was happening between his missionary and the young serviceman, released her from her mission a day early so she could dance with Charles.

After the conference Charles hitchhiked back to his base, his thoughts filled with Lucie. Three months later he was transferred to Liege, and he and Lucie began dating seriously. On October 14, 1961, when they were each twenty-six years old, they were married.

"I didn't get very far with my career," Sister Didier said in an interview soon after her husband was sustained as a General Authority. "I was just getting started and I was called on my mission. Two years later I started again with my career, but then I got married. That stopped me again, but I continued to sing. I had some concerts, but when the children came my family became my career because it was certainly more important." (*Church News*, October 25, 1975, p. 7.)

"Since our marriage, her singing has been done mainly in church buildings," adds Elder Didier. "She has some regrets about what she has given up, but she is a very devoted wife and mother and feels she has chosen the right path." They are the parents of two sons, Patrick and Marc, who both filled missions — in Chile and Ecuador — and are now married.

Elder and Sister Didier's life together has been a pattern of devoted church service. Over the years after their marriage, the Church in Europe grew and matured, due in part to the leadership of the Didiers and many other devoted members. Elder Didier served as branch president in Liege from 1964 to 1967, when he moved to Frankfurt, Germany, to work as assistant director of the Church's translation and distribution department there. Three years later he was called to serve as president of the Geneva Switzerland Mission, the first native European mission president who had not previously lived in the United States. In 1973 the Didiers returned to Frankfurt, where he became director of the translation and distribution department and was also called to serve as a regional representative.

The frequent moves presented many challenges for the family, especially their two sons. Each new setting meant a new culture, new school, new friends, and often a new language. "They had a very demanding youth. Moving so frequently gave them feelings of insecurity, inconsistency, and impermanence," says Elder Didier.

In late September 1975 Elder Didier traveled to Salt Lake City to attend a seminar for regional representatives, to be held in conjunction with general conference. On Tuesday, September 30, he received a phone call at his hotel from D. Arthur Haycock, secretary to President Spencer W. Kimball. Minutes later he found himself being taken to President Kimball's home, where he was greeted at the door by the prophet himself and his wife, Camilla.

President Kimball explained that the First Quorum of the Seventy, which would serve under the First Council of the Seventy, was to be organized at conference that weekend. Then he asked Elder Didier if he would become a member of that body.

"In a few seconds your whole future becomes blind. You put yourself in the hands of the Lord and do what he wants you to do," says Elder Didier. He accepted the calling immediately, and President Kimball opened his Doctrine and Covenants and began reading from section 107, teaching him about this new position.

On Thursday Brother Haycock asked Elder Didier, "Is your wife here? She has to be here." Elder Didier called her in Frankfurt, and she was able to get her visa in order and leave the next day. But her flight arrived in New York City late on Friday evening, so she missed the connection to Salt Lake City. She arrived at noon Saturday, too late to witness her husband's being sustained in the Saturday morning session of general conference, but she was present when he was set apart the next day.

"I think the Lord educated us carefully for this calling," Sister Didier said later. "I am an only child and very attached to my parents and country, but when I went on my own mission I became much more independent; and when my husband was called as mission president, I had the feeling in my heart that I should not really plan to go home again." (*Ensign*, November 1985, p. 136.)

And indeed, being on the Lord's errand has kept the Didiers moving all over the globe. Elder Didier's first assignment as a General Authority was to preside over the Europe West Area, headquartered in Brussels. He served there until 1979, when he was assigned to Canada for two years. In 1981 he went to the Uruguay/Paraguay/Argentina Area for three years, and in 1984 to Brazil. In 1985 he returned to the United States as president of the North American Southwest Area, and in 1987 he was appointed president over the South America North Area, which includes Bolivia, Peru, Ecuador, Venezuela, Colombia, French Guiana, Guyana, and Surinam.

"Being assigned in the states is very different from other places, such as South America," observes Elder Didier. "In the United States you have many second- and third-generation Latter-day Saints, while you rarely find that in South America. In Brazil, for example, there are now [1990] almost 350,000 members, 225,000 of whom have joined the Church in the last ten years. That gives you an idea of how hard it is to keep up with that massive growth in terms of leadership and training."

Living in so many different parts of the world, associating with a wide variety of people and cultures, and speaking six different languages has given Elder Didier a feeling of being an international emissary for the Lord, a citizen of the world rather than of a particular country. "Belgium is and will always be my country, but it is not my home," he explains. "Home is where my furniture is, where my family is, where my grandchildren are." For now, that is in Salt Lake City.

Although family and church are his main priorities, Elder Didier strives to maintain a balance in his life, which means spending as much free time as possible outdoors. His interests include such activities as gardening, racquetball, volleyball, table tennis, swimming, fishing, computer chess, and reading Church books, histories, and biographies. He enjoys attending movies, opera, and theater with his wife and painting with watercolors, most often doing reproductions of ancient American artifacts. A few of his paintings have recently been published on postcards.

After his calling as a Seventy, Elder Didier—like many others in his position—found himself asking, "Why? Why me?" It may be a question that deep soul-searching will never answer definitively, but it is one into which he has received some insight.

"Knowing that I was called by a prophet of God who believes I can do it has given me security and has made me feel very humble and eager to learn," he says. "Sometimes a window opens up and a little light is shed on your life and you are allowed to see a bit of your life in perspective. Looking back, I can see how I was prepared for something. I was always fond of languages, I have undergone a lot of maturity in Church experience, and I have been through a lot that could have left me inactive, but instead has served to strengthen my testimony. I have been led step by step in the gospel. If you recognize the opportunities as they come, you will grow from them; if you deny them, you lose the battle."

F. Enzio Busche

Picking his way through the debris, the thirteen-year-old youth stopped in horror before the smoking pile of rubble that had been his home just hours earlier. The night before, he had crouched in terror when thunder from hundreds of bombers rattled the glass and shook the walls and floors of his boarding school. From the windows he and his classmates could see flames leaping into the night sky, while acrid smoke seared their nostrils. They had gotten used to the air raids strafing Dortmund, Germany—American planes by day and British by night. But the attacks were getting closer and becoming more frequent, and he knew this last one had come perilously close to his home, just a few miles from the school. Now, gazing at the wreckage, he felt that everything that was solid and dependable—family, home, country, values—lay disintegrating in the ruins. Bitterness and hopelessness began to form a cold, hard lump in his chest that in time would expand and threaten his very life. As he struggled to comprehend the destruction before him, he had no way of knowing that the worst was still to come. Nothing in his early childhood had prepared him to deal with what he was going through.

Enzio Busche was born in Dortmund on April 5, 1930. Though the city was a tumultuous place of depression and unrest, Fritz Busche, owner of a small printing business, tried to create an idyllic environment for his family by building them a spacious stone house on ten acres of wooded countryside. Tall fences surrounded the property, creating a sheltered refuge where the Busche children — four daughters and a son — spent many happy hours playing with their animals, romping through the hills, and reading fairy tales and folk legends.

Fritz was familiar with the horrors of war. As a lieutenant in the German army in World War I, he was captured during the first days of fighting and spent almost four years in a prison camp in France. Though being removed from the fighting may have saved his life, he endured horrible conditions of filth, exposure, and starvation. These circumstances bound him and his fellow prisoners tightly together, and he became especially close to a soldier named Enzio, an Italian version of the name Henry. The two men made a pact that if they lived through their ordeal and ever married and had a family, each would name his first son after the other. "My father didn't really like the name Enzio much, but he was a man of honor who kept his word," says Elder Busche now. "Although the name is quite common in Italy, I have never heard of it for a German. I take it with pride because it is a monument to the integrity of my father." This same characteristic of honor bound Fritz to his family through the trials of another war and its accompanying separations and difficulties.

31

Aenne Weber was a beautiful doctor's helper when she met and married the shy thirty-five-year-old Fritz. Her mother had died when Aenne was twelve, and her father, a railroad worker, married a woman who made life very difficult for her stepdaughter. Seeking an escape from unbearable circumstances, Aenne left her small hometown soon after the marriage and went to Dortmund, where she managed to eke out a meager existence for several years. When she married Fritz Busche she gained a measure of security and love, though she was not able to completely lift the shadows from her childhood legacy of the lack of guidance and protection.

Enzio was her second child, and following his birth she became ill and had to have a nurse come to her home to help care for her and her children. This warmhearted woman, who never married, was nicknamed Tetta by the Busche children and became a permanent fixture in their household, waiting on Aenne and supplying maternal care and warmth to the children. She lived with the family until her death in 1974.

"Although as a child I was afraid of my mother, I now believe that considering her difficult youth, she was a wonderful mother with many caring and concerned attributes," explains Elder Busche. "She always avoided speaking of her past and would never reveal anything meaningful about her own upbringing, even to us. Whenever we asked her about it, she would say, 'I don't want to talk about it; there's nothing worth mentioning.'

"My parents didn't have what one would call a warm, close relationship, but because of my father's integrity and understanding of his responsibilities, he never argued with Mother and treated her always with a most loyal caring and loving respect. He never criticized her or allowed anyone else to say anything negative about her."

Despite the lack of significant affection from his mother, Enzio found security in his father's love and the order and discipline typical of a German family in the 1930s. This security was short-lived, however, for bombs began falling on Dortmund when Enzio was nine. Being so cloistered from the turmoil that was infesting Germany had left the young boy vulnerable and unprepared to deal with the realities of a nation rapidly rushing into war. His father was soon drafted into military service, and for years the family had no knowledge of his whereabouts. (Today a drawing by the nine-year-old Enzio hangs on a wall of his office in the Church Office Building in Salt Lake City. In vivid purple, yellow, and black, it dramatically depicts a city under siege, bombs dropping and exploding from low-flying planes, a grim reminder of a war that tore asunder his childish innocence and security.)

Now, with his home bombed and school disbanded, Enzio caught a train to the forest near Bad Kissingen, where his mother, sisters, and Tetta had sought refuge. The trip, which would normally have taken seven hours, lasted two days, as the train inched through rubble and detoured around blown-up track. A target of enemy fire, the train made repeated stops and passengers ran screaming into the woods, seeking protection among the trees from the air attacks. Reunited, the family fled to eastern and then southern Germany, where they lived in two small rooms, sharing a bathroom with six other families.

In March 1945, not yet fifteen years of age, Enzio was drafted into the army as the Third Reich made a desperate last-ditch attempt to rally strength. Dressed in his Hitler Youth uniform and sporting an unfamiliar weapon, he was called up immediately. He had to travel on foot, for the army had no transportation for the fourteen-year-old draftees.

"I was a little kid and scared to death," he recalled later. "We were under constant attack, but I never once shot back. I experienced terrible things that are beyond my ability to explain. In that chaos every emotion was loose and everyone behaved crazily. People panicked and shot themselves; nothing was illegal and there was no police protection. Money lost its value and people threw it away like dirty paper." The young troops, commanded by an eighteen-year-old, were soon running for their lives, hiding in the Bavarian forest on the Czechoslovakian border and foraging for food.

The confused, inexperienced soldiers were captured by American troops and herded into a barn. They spent three days in the makeshift prison, crowded so tightly they could neither sit nor lie down, and, although many hadn't eaten in days, without food. Then they were transferred to a prison camp, where their captors, short of supplies themselves, released for an hour a day prisoners under the age of sixteen and sent them out to beg or scavenge for food. Because of previous indoctrination, Enzio expected to be executed at the camp. Instead, with the end of the war in sight and supplies dangerously low, prisoners who would swear to never again take up arms were released within three weeks. Although more than happy to take the oath, he found freedom did not improve his circumstances, for he had neither transportation nor provisions. After a grueling journey, he was at last reunited with his mother and sisters. His father's whereabouts were unknown at the time; later it was discovered he had been in Belgium in a British prison camp.

During the summer of 1945, Enzio made his way back to the ruins of the family home. Dortmund, an industrial center, had been bombed continuously from 1939 to 1945, and Enzio returned to a demolished city where great numbers of people died daily of starvation and disease. Neighbors who had returned to the city earlier had planted gardens on the Busche property and now shared potatoes and other vegetables with him.

One by one the family members returned to the city. Fritz Busche, Enzio's father, was finally released in the summer of

1947. Living in the rubble of their house for the next three years, the Busches struggled to rebuild their home, city, and lives. Fortunately they were able to breed five sheep to provide milk and meat, to supplement what the land would yield. A blessing in disguise had come just before the end of the war when a supply train was riddled with bullets by fighter planes. Sticky molasses came pouring out of the train cars like water through a sieve, and the residents had caught it in every available container. This supply helped sustain them through a very difficult time.

With the war ended, the barbarous acts of the Hitler regime came to light, to the horror of the German people. "People don't believe it when I say that we had no idea what was going on, but it's true," says Elder Busche. "It's difficult to understand unless you have lived in a state where all of the information you get, beyond your own neighborhood, is controlled by the government. To us, the Nazi regime, the National Socialist party, was held up as a model of honesty and integrity, industry and caring for the poor; we were taught those values at home and in school. To be a member of the Hitler Youth organization meant you had ideals and standards, much like being a Boy Scout in America. We did hear a few rumors about what was going on, but they were so absurd that no one believed them. When my father found out about the atrocities done in the name of Germany, he was so devastated he could hardly breathe."

Enzio was likewise deeply disturbed as he became aware of the immoral foundations of which he and his fellow countrymen were a part. He returned to school the year after the war ended, but soon found himself questioning life itself. Studying Latin vocabularies seemed absurd and trivial to a young man who had experienced so much devastation and chaos. All of the values he had been taught before the war, based on Hitler's philosophies, now proved to be a sham.

Teachers who had taught the Nazi doctrines now denied any knowledge of them. If adults didn't know the difference between right and wrong, who did? Whom could he follow? What could he believe in that wouldn't prove false? Did life hold any meaning? As he searched for answers, he plunged into a deep, lengthy melancholia.

During the period when Enzio and his family were in exile in southern Germany, he had had an experience that would profoundly affect his life. Lying in bed one night, sick with fear and confusion and terrified that his father would be killed or was already dead, he recalls, he "had a most frightening thought: What is the purpose of my being here on this earth? I could not answer this question and it led right into another one that was even more frightening: What is eternity? I looked into my heart for the answers to these questions, but the more I thought about eternity, the more lost I felt. There was nothing to hold onto, nothing to stand on. I had the feeling of falling, falling, falling without stopping. It scared me terribly.

"I was awake until early in the morning, and I was so overcome with despair that I began to cry. I wept and wept. Then suddenly something changed. A comforting power enveloped me, and a small voice said to my soul, 'Don't be scared. You are my child. Have trust in Me.' Immediately sadness left me and joy and happiness filled my heart. All my fear, loneliness, and despair were changed into feelings of warmth and comfort. That night I learned for the first time that there is some unseen but loving person who is concerned about us."

But this experience wasn't sufficient to sustain the young man as he grew into adulthood, and his searching for answers continued. After he completed high school, he studied at universities in Bonn and Freiburg, received vocational training in Bonn and Stuttgart, and then began working in his father's printing business, which was doing very well in post-war Germany. He also began thinking about getting married.

Enzio had been in love for eighteen years with the beautiful Jutta Baum, whom he had met for the first time when he was seven years old. He had erected an elaborate cathedral of building blocks when a neighbor came to visit his mother, bringing her two-year old daughter, Jutta, with her. Immediately on entering the room, the little girl went over to the cathedral and demolished it with a single, well-aimed kick. Aenne Busche, proud of her son's work, was visibly upset. But Enzio was taken with the little stranger and told his mother, "Don't worry, it is fine."

"I can still remember that there was something remarkable about her. She was adorable. It was already love," he says now, a smile lighting his blue eyes.

In 1955, when he was twenty-five and she was twenty, they were married. But though they were deeply in love, he found that their relationship didn't provide the answers for the question that still haunted him. In some ways marriage only deepened his dilemma because he was not alone anymore—he now felt responsibility for another human being. Different expectations and temperaments left the couple feeling little sense of unity, with the threat of drifting into isolation from one another. Three months after their marriage, Enzio became seriously ill. The doctors' diagnosis was that he had an incurable liver disease, and he was hospitalized with a dangerously high blood/bilirubin count and a frightening greenish pallor.

"As I lay in bed, I began to realize the nearness of the end of my earthly experience and was overwhelmed by a panic-like fear," he explains. "I saw myself in all my nakedness, unprotected, and feeling the heavy burden of my sins. Not that I considered myself a big sinner, but even small sins—like the lack of gratitude for fresh air to breathe, the lack of gratitude for my parents' care, or the memory of every lightminded joke or mannerism—began to burden me. I felt unprepared, unready to die, and that it was completely impossible to go to the other side without someone to help, someone to speak for me. I saw the absolute need for a Redeemer." As he struggled in this situation, he resolved that if he could come back to life he would "live to become a different person, a person that has seen that man will be judged by his every thought and deed."

Exactly one week later, on a day that he believed would surely be his last on earth, he lay alone. His family, unable to continue to witness his great pain and despair, had left; and the doctors, believing that nothing more could be done for him, had turned off the life-support systems. What happened next was something he feels "completely inadequate" to put into words. "On the left corner of the ceiling was suddenly a flash of light, brilliant and white, and so intimidating and strong that it scared me totally," he explains. Then a voice, "speaking loud and clear," told him, "When you can pray now, you will recover."

Realizing that this voice was real and had a power and authority that surpassed anything he had ever known before, he felt a compelling need to pray. But he felt that the only prayer he knew—the Lord's Prayer, which he had memorized in school—was inadequate. "After some time of wrestling, something or someone helped me to utter perhaps the most honorable prayer anyone can pray, 'Dein wille geschehe' ('Thy will be done')," he recalls. "In the moment I finished this prayer, the whole situation of my life changed. It turned from despair, agony, and fear into the most indescribable joy I could imagine. I wanted to jump and dance, sing and shout, though my body was so weak I could not move. But I knew without a shadow of a doubt that I would recover."

As a result of this experience, Enzio made two further

commitments that changed the course of his life. First, he would never deny the experience and would testify of its reality. Second, he vowed to go to the ends of the earth, if necessary, to find the source of this power and then to ask whether he would be permitted to become a disciple of it.

"I feel like I have lived on borrowed time every day since this experience," Elder Busche says now. "I feel a tremendous urgency to testify of the power that I felt and of the absolute necessity for a Redeemer to intercede on our behalf. I wish I could say that I've lived up to those commitments, but I've tried, and I am still trying."

He began to recover rapidly, to the amazement of his doctors and nurses. A week later, as blood test results began to dramatically improve, they admitted that he did indeed have a chance to survive. One doctor later admitted that he had never known of anyone living after having blood counts as high as Enzio's had been, and that his recovery was technically impossible. But when Enzio's father insisted that an exploratory operation be performed, the surgeons found a liver that was unscarred and bore no effects of the ailment, which normally would have seriously damaged the organ.

Enzio, wasting no time in trying to identify the power he had experienced, asked Jutta to bring him a Bible. Although shocked by his uncharacteristic request, she complied, and he voraciously read the book from cover to cover, stopping only to eat and sleep. As a result, he gained a powerful testimony of Jesus Christ and of the words of God contained in that book.

For five months he convalesced in a Catholic hospital, gazing often at a crucifix on the wall of his room. He was also impressed by the head nurse, a nun who worked up to sixteen hours a day, seven days a week. He admired the loving, joyful goodness that seemed to flow from her as she accomplished even the most menial chores, commenting that "it seemed impossible not to feel good in her presence."

One day he told her he wanted to become a disciple of Jesus Christ and asked if the Catholic Church was the true church of God. A faraway look came into her eyes and after a long pause she told him, "No, it is not. You are looking for the living Christ, but the Catholic Church is a church of dead traditions." Later he asked her how many Christian churches there were. When she guessed maybe three hundred, he answered casually, "Two hundred and ninety-nine to go."

As soon as Enzio left the hospital and was able to get out, he visited the minister of the local Lutheran congregation. After explaining what he was looking for, he told the minister, "I want to live a different life. What can I do?" The surprised minister at first told him to see a psychiatrist, but then, convinced of the young man's sincerity, counseled Enzio to attend meetings of the church regularly. Later the minister asked him to visit the parishioners and see if he could persuade more of them to come to meetings. In talking to his neighbors about religion, Enzio became aware of how many of his questions weren't answered by Lutheran doctrines. He looked into various other churches and doctrines but still couldn't find what he was looking for.

One evening, filled with frustration and longing, he and Jutta knelt in supplication, "this time not simply repeating the Lord's Prayer, but daring to utter words of our own. We asked, 'Father, are you there? Can you hear us? We want to live different lives. We want to find your church. Even if it is small; even if its members are persecuted; even if they are driven out of the countries as they have been before, we want to find them.' As we were praying, again that wonderful peace came into my heart."

One morning about three weeks later, the only weekday morning of that year that Enzio was at home, the doorbell rang. Two young men in dark suits and white shirts were standing there. When they told him they were from a church and mentioned the name, he responded, "Whoever sent you, tell your boss the name of the church is too long. It isn't good for sales." But he did listen to them, and, although he was unimpressed by their foreign-sounding message, he was deeply touched by the young men themselves. There was something about them that was totally different from anyone he had ever known before. They had the kind of spirit Enzio and Jutta hoped their own children would possess when they became adults. He was particularly impressed with the honor and respect with which the young men spoke of their parents.

Once introduced to the gospel, Enzio didn't accept it easily. The doctrines, like the messengers, were a contrast from anything he had heard before, totally different from what he had been expecting to find. He spent the next two years earnestly investigating the Church before he was at last convinced of its truthfulness. "There is nothing more unbearable than the truth," he says now. "It is so unwanted, so unpleasant, because when we find it we must change. It took me nearly two years before I could not find any escape, any more excuses for not being baptized."

At last he was ready, but he didn't want to be baptized without his wife. Jutta had long before been touched by the spirit of the young elders, but had busied herself in another room during their long conversations with her husband. Now she listened intently, and after only three meetings—much to her husband's amazement—she had a testimony and was ready for baptism. "I don't know why you've had to study two years," she told him. "This is nothing new. It is what I have always believed since I was a girl."

At the time Enzio was surprised to discover this spiritual capacity in his wife, but now he explains, "Women obviously have an easier access to spiritual understandings than men

41

do. Even now I have to read, study, and ponder the scriptures intensely every day to stay on the same spiritual level as that which comes naturally to her."

Enzio and Jutta were baptized on January 19, 1958, in a public swimming pool. At the time they had one son, Markus, and Jutta was pregnant with their second, Matthias. Maja, their daughter, was born two years later, and Daniel three years after that. The little family found that membership in The Church of Jesus Christ of Latter-day Saints revolutionized their lives, alienating them from family and friends and their previous life-style. Although Enzio's father encouraged him to follow his convictions, his mother had difficulty accepting the change and became somewhat outspoken in her ridicule and criticism.

Despite these obstacles, Enzio and Jutta were finally at peace. The message of the restored gospel answered all of their questions and gave them purpose in their marriage and in their lives. They began attending a tiny branch in Dortmund and Enzio was immediately drawn into various callings, serving as branch secretary, then elders quorum president, and teaching in the Young Men's Mutual Improvement Association and the Sunday School. He subsequently served as a branch president, district president, counselor to two mission presidents, and regional representative. Favorite callings of both Elder and Sister Busche have been those involved with youth and missionaries.

During the time Elder Busche was growing through church service, he was also growing into a respected businessman, becoming co-owner of Busche Printing in 1955 and sole owner eight years later when his father died. Eventually the firm became one of the largest offset printing and publishing companies in Germany, with many subsidiaries and partnerships. He credits much of his professional success to spiritual influence of the Holy Ghost, explaining, "I have not made a single decision, whether it be knocking on a customer's door or leading a business meeting, without asking the Lord. Without that, I would have failed miserably."

At the age of seventy-three, Fritz Busche had a heart attack. When Enzio visited him in the hospital, the attending doctors assured him that his father could expect a complete recovery. As the father and son talked, their conversation became intimate and, in a rare burst of candor, Fritz said, "Can you promise me that you will never leave your church?"

"I was so startled to hear those words that I could barely contain my joy," remembers Elder Busche. "I had no idea he felt that way. 'Why?' I asked him. And he replied, 'Everything in you that was good has become better since you joined that church. But more important, you became a happy person. I believe that as long as you stay true to your religion, things will go well with you.' " That was the last conversation Enzio had with his father, for Fritz had a second heart attack and died a few days later.

"My father has been the greatest influence in my life because of his sense of responsibility for his family and his fellowman," explains Elder Busche. "I remember a particular incident when the German government wanted to bestow on him a high merit medal for his business success and civic example. He became furious and turned it down, saying 'Nobody is living good enough in this world to receive a merit medal.' He was more concerned with his deeds and attitudes than in taking pride in the honors of the world."

Several months after his father's death, Enzio was sleeping when he had a "very powerful spiritual experience that was more than a dream." He saw himself sitting in his office when a knock came at the door and a young man whom he didn't know opened it. The person said in an authoritative voice, "We are ready." Just as Enzio was about to ask what these words meant, he saw his father standing just behind the man.

"My father had a sincere, intense expression on his face, as if this were the most urgent moment of his whole existence," recalls Elder Busche. "It was as if he were very concerned, and I saw that he was not allowed to enter the room, but he had to stand outside with the look of a humble beggar. It hurt me that he would have to beg something from me." The man repeated the words "We are ready," and then the two figures were gone.

"This was a sacred witness to me that my father was ready to commit to the yoke of Christ," Elder Busche testifies. "I have since had a very compelling spiritual witness that he has accepted the work we have done for him and that many of my ancestors on the other side have also embraced the gospel."

When the Busches joined the Church, the Dortmund Branch met in an old, rundown school in a less than desirable neighborhood. It later moved to an apartment above a clothing store in an equally unsuitable area. By then Enzio was serving as branch president. He and the other members dreamed of building a new chapel, but land in the city was very difficult to purchase, especially for members of an unpopular religion. After fighting legal battles for years and being stymied at every turn, the frustrated Saints didn't know where to turn for help. The president of the mission promised them that if they would commit to achieving 100 percent in their home teaching, the Lord would perform a miracle. Within months, they were consistently reaching their 100 percent goal.

About that time a man with an interesting story came to see President Busche. During World War II, the man said, he had been incarcerated in an American prisoner of war camp. The captain of the camp was a Mormon who taught him the basic principles of self-confidence, happiness, and success. The former POW said that as a result, he owed everything he had, including his very life, to that Mormon captain. He also said that recently he had felt the necessity of repaying the captain. Because he was unable to remember the soldier's name, he had decided to see if there were Mormons in Dortmund and to do something for them. When President Busche told him they were trying to obtain property for a chapel, the man replied that would be easy, for he was the head of the city's real estate department—the very official whom President Busche had been blocked many times from seeing!

In the civic offices the following day, President Busche pointed on the city map to a few sites, each in a humble location, where the chapel might be erected. But the city official moved President Busche's finger to the most beautiful part of the city and, looking up with a smile, asked, "Where is your faith?" Because of this man's influence, the Church was able to purchase, at a minimal price, a choice piece of land where a beautiful chapel was eventually built.

A Church program in effect at that time allowed the members to build the chapel themselves. "As we worked on the chapel, the children in the neighborhood would gather and watch us," Elder Busche recalls. Then one day a girl about ten or eleven years old came by carrying a petition.

"What is that petition?" President Busche asked.

"Don't you know?" she responded. "The Lutheran minister doesn't like you and has called a town meeting for tomorrow night. He hopes to stir up the people against you to tear down your walls. But don't worry," she assured him. "We children on this street will stand in a line, and they will have to run us down before they can get to the chapel."

Several of the Saints, including their branch president, decided to attend the meeting and sit in the front row, but not to say anything unless specifically instructed to do so by the Spirit. When the minister declared that the Mormons didn't believe in Christ's atonement, President Busche, who had received a special witness on that very subject and vowed to testify of it, knew this was the time.

As he rose to his feet and started to speak, several people complained that his voice wasn't loud enough, so the minister invited him to come to the pulpit. Under the influence of the Spirit, he spoke on the atonement for about thirty minutes, and many in the audience wept openly as he finished. As a result, construction on the chapel continued unobstructed and many people who had attended the meeting requested more information about the Church. Several were eventually baptized.

In 1977 Elder Busche, who had been a regional representative since 1970, was serving as a translator for President Spencer W. Kimball at a conference in West Berlin. About ten o'clock one evening President Kimball met with him in the stake president's office and called him to become a member of the First Quorum of the Seventy.

"I think the Lord helps by not giving you the full understanding at the time," said Elder Busche later. "If you really understood all that it meant, you wouldn't be able to respond." But after a long pause he did respond, saying, "I can't see an honest way to escape."

"Could you put that in a positive way?" President Kimball asked.

Elder Busche's answer was an unequivocal yes, which he has been reaffirming daily ever since. His first assignment as a General Authority was as president of the Germany Munich Mission. Two years later he was released from that calling and moved with his family to Church headquarters in Salt Lake City. He served as president of the Frankfurt Germany Temple from 1987 to 1989, with Sister Busche serving as temple matron, and then became assistant executive director of the Temple Department and first counselor in the presidency of the North America Northeast Area.

In addition to his awareness of the spiritual dimensions of life, Elder Busche is committed to physical fitness. At age thirty-nine he suffered a circulatory breakdown, which he attributed, in part, to a sedentary life-style. After his recovery, he and Sister Busche began to jog regularly in the forests near their home, and eventually he set up a jogging program in which runners could meet and run various routes and distances together. That program has been adopted by the German Sportive Organization and is used throughout the country. For many years Elder Busche ran up to thirty miles per week, occasionally running as much as twenty miles at a time. Although he doesn't have as much time for jogging as he used to, he still enjoys vigorous walking and long-distance hiking. "It leads a man to himself and often to self-analysis and necessary corrections," he explains.

Elder Busche is an example of the miraculous healing power of the gospel. The bitter, melancholic young man who experienced the brutality of war and the depravity of the human spirit has become a servant and disciple of the Lord Jesus Christ. He is daily striving to keep the vows he made to the Lord more than thirty years ago, when he lay near death, and to let the sacred power that he found as a result be the influence by which he measures his life. In answering the Lord's calls to serve, he has left all that was familiar— culture, language, home, business, and country—but in a totally different way than he anticipated. "The Lord has not allowed me to sacrifice," he says. "Every time I have been ready to do so, he has given me additional blessings that are beyond my comprehension.

"Being allowed to serve is never a sacrifice, but a great privilege," he concludes. "When we are truly converted, we don't see the Lord's work as a burden, but as a privilege. Being allowed to serve is not a sacrifice, it's a joy."

YOSHIHIKO KIKUCHI

Lying on the massive desk are several sheets of white paper stapled together, the pages worn and the corners creased from being turned often. It is a list of names, addresses, and phone numbers, some highlighted in yellow or pink, others crossed out. Here or there a name or a phone number has been penciled in or circled. A man sits at the desk, a telephone pressed to his ear, and methodically goes down the roster, calling each name in turn. His cheerful countenance brightens even more as a voice is heard on the other end.

"Hello?"

"Hello. Sister Olsen?"

"Yes."

"This is Brother Kikuchi, your son's mission president in Hawaii."

A split second of silence and then a rush of words: "What's wrong? Has something happened? How is he?"

"Everything's fine," he quickly reassures her. "This is not one of those kinds of calls. I just want to tell you thank you, thank you for raising such a beautiful son. Elder Olsen is a dedicated, good missionary and he's having wonderful success."

"That's so good to hear." This time the worried tone is replaced by one of gratitude.

"Thank you for sending him on a mission," he continues. "It means so much to many who now have the gospel because of families like yours and missionaries like your son, like the elders who came to my door in Japan and taught me the gospel. Now your son is finding other Kikuchis—or other Camargos, or other Busches, or Youngs, or Smiths—who are so blessed by the missionaries and their parents' prayers." The conversation continues, every comment punctuated by Elder Kikuchi's expressions of appreciation. When he hangs up ten minutes later he is laughing, a happy sound borne of sheer delight in the thankfulness he feels at being a member of the Church and the joy of being able to share both that gratitude and the gospel with others.

"When I come to Salt Lake for general conference, I like to call my missionaries' parents and tell them thank you for raising such good, wonderful sons and daughters," he explains. "The parents are surprised to hear from me, but that's my greatest joy, to express my appreciation to my brothers and sisters." This overwhelming feeling of gratitude is as much a part of Elder Kikuchi's being as his infectious grin, his five-foot eight-inch frame, or his total dedication to the Lord.

It is a dedication that has transformed his life—transcending time and events, boundaries and cultures, prejudice and hatred—and filled his existence with the rich abundance that

49

only Christ-centered living can bring. As the first native-born Japanese General Authority (his colleague, Elder Adney Y. Komatsu, is of Japanese descent but was born in Hawaii), Elder Kikuchi carries a three-pronged message to individuals and congregations throughout the world: the gospel is universal in scope and purpose, Latter-day Saints must live righteously and send their sons and daughters on missions and go themselves, and Jesus Christ is the author of the gospel and his message must be preached to every nation with great urgency.

The strength and power in the testimony borne by this humble servant of the Lord belie his modest beginnings in rural Japan. The Church, which had earlier found meager response in tradition-steeped Japan, had all but disappeared from the country during the 1930s. Japan grew increasingly anti-American, and by 1941, the year of his birth, the missionaries had been gone for nearly a decade. Thus, the chances that Yoshihiko Kikuchi would subsequently encounter emissaries from the Church were miniscule.

Yoshihiko was born in Horoizumi, the "snow country" of Hokkaido, at the tip of a peninsula in northern Japan. Though the island nation was teetering on the verge of war, the impending conflict had little effect on the childish world of Yoshihiko. The third child born to Hatsuo and Koyo Ikeda Kikuchi, he already had an older brother and sister, and eventually would have a younger sister as well.

The family was well-to-do, for Hatsuo owned a fleet of fishing ships. Hatsuo was by turn both a strict disciplinarian and an affectionate father. Yoshihiko recollects the strictly enforced early-morning ritual of kneeling on tatami mats, forehead touching the floor, and vowing to be a good boy and to show great respect for his parents — and being thrown barefooted into the snow one morning for not complying. He also remembers being squeezed tightly in his father's arms, and the itchy feeling of his father's beard on his tender skin.

But such memories of his father are few, for soon the harsh claws of World War II tore into Yoshihiko's secure, ordered world. Hatsuo enlisted in the army and one day he was home recuperating from an illness when he decided to go out on one of his fishing vessels. While he was at sea, American bombers attacked the fleet, killing many, including Hatsuo. Yoshihiko's final memories of his father are of a large funeral attended by a sizeable crowd, as befitted a great and respected man, and being told by one of the mourners that his father had been killed by an American bomb. Though he was too young to fully understand at the time, the seeds of hatred and prejudice had been planted in his heart and would grow as he did.

The tragedy changed the Kikuchi family's circumstances considerably. Koyo, a heartbroken young widow living far from her childhood home and relatives, found herself bound by tradition and respect for her husband to stay and care for his home and land, property that had been in his family for generations. Although she was forced to sell the fishing business to pay off debts and compensate the families of the others who died, she did retain four acres of farmland and about twenty-five wooded acres on a mountainside.

The family became practically self-sufficient, growing as much of their own food as possible, and raising sheep, pigs, chickens, and rabbits. To get much-needed cash, they sold firewood cut from their mountain acreage. Koyo also obtained a license to harvest *konbu* (tangle) and other seaweed, and until her first son became old enough to take over the chore, she hired a man to take his boat out in the ocean to cut the long strands, which were sold for food, glue, and starch. The children would also catch fish, which their mother dried and then sold in the village. But all of these activities produced a meager living at best, and Koyo often had to clean houses for extra income.

With his mother busy and his older brother and sister holding part-time jobs, Yoshihiko often found himself cooking the meals and keeping the house and yard tidy. It was also his job to keep the big Chinese vase in the kitchen filled with water, carried by bucket from an outside well. Before school he would often help with the weeding, watering, and fertilizing in the garden, and on spring mornings he helped gather the seaweed that had washed up on the beach, which the family would dry and sell.

Despite the responsibilities and hardships, Yoshihiko's childhood was generally happy. He found time to fish, swim, and surf in the ocean, and in the wintertime he enjoyed skiing on homemade skis made from curved tree branches. School was within walking distance, and he was a good student with an innate love of learning.

"We were a very close family," he remembers. "We went on picnics and other outings, and my mother would gather us around for a family night about once a week to talk about our father, our family, our ancestors, our future, and school. I am glad she taught me so many wonderful things. One thing in particular I remember her repeating is 'Behavior of others is greatest teacher—learn from them.' The toughest time was when I would see other boys playing baseball or something with their fathers. I still miss not having a father around. Had he lived, though, I don't believe he or I would ever have joined the Church. We would have had no reason to leave our hometown, and there is no way we would have come in contact with the Church in Horoizumi.

"I left my town, I can see now, because the Spirit was hunting for me," he adds. "In the scriptures it is recorded, 'I will send for many fishers . . . and they shall fish them; and after will I send for many hunters, and they shall hunt them from every mountain, and from every hill, and out of the holes of the rocks.' [Jeremiah 16:16.] I was hunted from my small town of Horoizumi."

Fate "hunted" for Yoshihiko by taking him away from home at the age of fifteen. He had just graduated from junior high school, and although he had a scholarship to pay the tuition for senior high school, he felt obligated to get a job and contribute to the family income. But he had difficulty finding work, and when he finally did, it was in the city of Muroran about twelve hours by train and bus from Horoizumi. There he worked in a family-owned shop that manufactured tofu (bean curd) and lived in the back of the store. He maintained a grueling schedule — rising at 4:30 A.M., working twelve to fourteen hours in the shop, and attending school at night — and he was desperately homesick.

After almost a year the stress and demands on his time affected the youth's health, and he was hospitalized after collapsing from exhaustion at work one day. This forced respite compelled him to slow down and brought on an uncharacteristic bout of loneliness and depression. He was sick, weary, afraid, and a long way from home. "Are you there?" he cried out in pain to the Lord from his hospital bed. "Do you know that I am here? Please help me!"

Finally his doctors told him there was little more they could do, and he was released from the hospital. They recommended a long recuperation period, but he didn't want to return home. "I thought at the time that I wanted to stay in Muroran to finish school," he says. His uncle, who lived in the city, agreed to let his nephew stay with him and his family and also arranged for him to take an employment examination in his company, a ship manufacturer. Yoshihiko passed the test and was asked to begin working in the company as soon as he was well enough. He could work in the mornings, attend the company school in the afternoons to be trained as an engineer, and live in the company dormitory.

It was during one of the long days Yoshihiko spent alone in his uncle's home recovering that two Americans knocked on the door. "Go home," he told them. "You killed my father. I don't like to see you."

One of them asked, "How old are you?" When he told them he was fifteen, they responded, "We would like to tell you a story of a boy just like you who saw Heavenly Father and the Lord Jesus Christ."

"Just a few weeks before I had been in the hospital praying, desperately seeking something," recalls Elder Kikuchi, "and so the name 'Heavenly Father' touched a chord inside of me and I just couldn't refuse. 'OK, I'll give you a few minutes,' I told them.

"There in my uncle's home, with no one else around, they told me the most wonderful story about Joseph Smith, and right then something went through my whole body. The harp strings of my soul started vibrating with a warm feeling. Now, of course, I know it was the Spirit. I just could not resist." After the missionaries bore their testimonies, one of them asked him to pray. He told them he didn't know how, and they wrote down the four steps for him to follow. The three young men knelt together, and Yoshihiko offered a humble, untried prayer to his Heavenly Father. It was the most spiritual experience of his life to that time. "That warm feeling spread through my whole soul and all the faculties of my body, and I just couldn't stop crying," he says.

At that moment everything was forever changed. The heart of a fatherless boy, scarred by bitterness and sorrow, was touched by two humble missionaries and the transcendent, healing love of Christ. Almost twenty-five years later Elder Kikuchi was to testify before a Churchwide audience, "Oh, how glorious is the power of the gospel which can change the hearts of people from sorrow and despair to happiness and joy!" (*Ensign*, November 1981, p. 70.)

After that, he couldn't learn the gospel fast enough, and he started dropping by the missionaries' apartment to be taught. "I was eating it up like a thirsty sponge, like water poured on dry desert soil."

Yoshihiko wanted to be baptized, and he called his mother for her permission. She told him no. "Why do you want to join the enemy's church, an *American* church?" she asked. "Do you know what they did to your father? How could you do this?"

He hung up the phone like the obedient son he was, but two days later he called again. "Please, Mother. I am so determined."

"You are too young to make this decision. You need to study more."

He told her he had been fasting and praying that she would let him join this church. When he explained to her what that meant, he could hear her upset, confused sobs over the phone. "Why, oh why, do you have to do this?" she moaned. Finally she asked, "Are you really serious about this?"

When he assured her he was, she said, "Son, if you really want this, you may do it." Then she gave him some counsel he cherishes to this day: "If you are really going to become a member of this church, you must see it through. Don't quit right in the middle."

"You know, I am not through yet," Elder Kikuchi reflects, his voice trembling with emotion. "My road is not yet at an end. But I feel a great assurance from my mother, and I cannot go against what she said. That was a turning point. I could have missed all of these blessings. If I had insisted that the missionaries go away, if they had not been so persistent, I wouldn't be here today. I am so grateful for this everlasting, most transcendent gospel that I can share with my wife and family and with my people and the other people of the world. This is my life; this is my blood; this is my way, my desire, my hope, and my dreams. To be in the service of my Savior is everything."

Yoshihiko was baptized on April 13, 1958, at age fifteen, and since then he has missed attending church only one Sunday. Soon after his baptism he moved into the dormitory of the ship manufacturer, and there, through his influence, several of his roommates joined the Church. Three years later, after he graduated from senior high school—and against the wishes of company management—he fulfilled a cherished dream by serving a full-time mission among his fellow Japanese.

After Elder Kikuchi had been in the mission field about a year, he attended a zone conference in Fukuoka, on the southern island of Kyushu. Elder Gordon B. Hinckley, recently called to the Council of the Twelve, presided. Elder Kikuchi, the only Japanese elder present, spoke very little English at the time and so missed most of what was said during the day-long workshops. At the end of the day a testimony meeting was held. After all of the other missionaries had borne their testimonies, Elder Hinckley asked Elder Kikuchi to bear his in Japanese. As soon as his companion translated the request, Elder Kikuchi stood up and began speaking in Japanese. While he was testifying, suddenly his soul was illuminated by the sweet feelings of the Spirit and love for the Lord, and he began to bear a heartfelt testimony— in English. Afterwards he couldn't remember what he had said, but he could remember vividly the feelings he was trying to communicate. Elder Hinckley got up and stated that although it was unusual for him to do so publicly, he wanted to give the young Japanese elder a blessing.

"I knew he was talking to me," says Elder Kikuchi, "but

didn't know what he was saying." Several of those present, including his companion and the mission president's wife, made notes on Elder Hinckley's blessing and gave them to him later, scraps of paper that he cherishes to this day.

"He blessed me that if I remained humble and faithful in the Lord's kingdom, and would dedicate myself to the course of truth and complete my education after my mission, the Lord would make me mighty and strong and would prepare me to assist his Zion to be established in this part of his vineyard. Many years later when I was called to serve in the First Quorum of the Seventy, I mentioned the incident to President Hinckley. He said that he remembered the episode, adding, 'I can recall how strong the spirit was that day.' " This incident, in addition to being a pivotal moment in Elder Kikuchi's life, marked the beginning of a long-lasting relationship between him and Elder Hinckley. The two had many opportunities to associate as Church business took Elder Hinckley to the Orient more than forty-five times during the next several years.

The incident also confirmed to Elder Kikuchi the importance of studying English in order to be better prepared for the work the Lord had in store for him. As he studied, his English became quite fluent, and years later, while serving in the presidencies of the Tokyo Mission and the Tokyo Stake, he often translated for visiting General Authorities.

After he had served in the mission field two years, Elder Kikuchi was asked by his mission president to stay six months more and prepare manuals in Japanese on basic leadership qualities and Church administrative procedures. At the end of that time the mission president called him in again and asked if he would like to be further blessed. "How much longer do you want me to stay?" asked Elder Kikuchi. This time it was a twelve-month extension to help in building new chapels. At the end of his three-and-a-half-year mission, Elder

Kikuchi was "anxious to get home because my fiancée was waiting. She had waited the entire time and not given up on me. I guess she felt something," he adds.

He met Toshiko Koshiya about a month after he joined the Church. She had been baptized a few years earlier after studying the gospel for almost two years. Two weeks after he returned from his mission, they were married civilly. Over the next two years they scrimped and saved to purchase tickets on a plane chartered for a temple excursion with fellow Japanese Latter-day Saints. Finally they and their baby daughter, Sarah, were sealed for eternity in the Hawaiian Temple.

Although Yoshihiko wanted to attend Brigham Young University and, through the help of his mission president, had a sponsor willing to help him, he and Toshiko prayed about the move and received the answer that the Lord wanted him to stay in his homeland. Soon the new husband and father was a student at a university in Tokyo, a sales employee, and president of the Tokyo West Branch. "I feel guilty if I'm not busy all of the time," he admits. And busy he was, with only about four hours of sleep a night, though he remembers those years as among the most rewarding and fruitful of his life.

Shortly after this he was called to serve as counselor to the mission president, and soon after, in the spring of 1970, Elders Ezra Taft Benson and Gordon B. Hinckley organized the first stake in Japan and called Elder Kikuchi to be first counselor in the stake presidency, at twenty-six the youngest officer in the Tokyo Japan Stake.

The next few years marked a time of growth and stability for the Kikuchis and the Church in Japan. They had three daughters and a son, he was serving as president of the Tokyo Stake, and his international firm had promoted him to sales manager for the entire country. But the time had come when the Lord had another setting in mind for this servant.

At the end of September 1977, Elder Kikuchi was just returning to work after a two-week illness. He returned home about midnight one evening and was told that the First Presidency had been trying to contact him. Although he was tired and hungry, he was about to return the call immediately when the phone rang. It was D. Arthur Haycock, secretary to President Spencer W. Kimball. They spoke for a few moments and then President Kimball came on the line. He inquired about Brother Kikuchi's health, his family, and his business, and then he asked, "Are you coming to conference?" Elder Kikuchi replied that he wasn't scheduled to come until the following April.

President Kimball asked again, "Are you coming to conference?"

"This conference, President?"

"Yes, I'd like to see you. Could you leave this afternoon? Call me when you get in."

The next few days became a whirlwind of frustration and obstacles for the Kikuchis. They found that their passports and visas had expired, and, since it was a holiday weekend, it would be almost impossible to obtain the necessary documents. But somehow they managed to get the paperwork taken care of and to tie up some business problems and stake obligations. They missed one plane and almost missed another one because of traffic tie-ups. And on arriving in the United States, Sister Kikuchi discovered, to their dismay, that her purse, full of credit cards, her passport, and hundreds of dollars, had been left in the Tokyo Airport. (It was later returned, all contents intact.) When they finally arrived in Salt Lake City Thursday evening, they had missed their scheduled appointment with President Kimball, and it was quickly changed to six o'clock the next morning.

Early Friday morning President Kimball greeted them warmly with a hug and a kiss and asked about their trip. "I couldn't tell him it was awful, even though it was," recalls Elder Kikuchi, shaking his head. After inquiring about their family, business, ward, and stake, President Kimball leaned back in his chair and said, "The Lord has called you to serve as a General Authority of the Church. Would you accept the call?"

The words rushed over the couple like a powerful wave. "I knew what he was saying, but I couldn't comprehend it," says Elder Kikuchi. "We had thought of many reasons he might want to see us, but had never, never imagined it would be this. I asked him to repeat what he had said, and he kindly said the same words. My wife and I both broke down and cried, not because we were happy but because" — he pauses — " . . . *me?* A General Authority? The General Authorities are . . . " Elder Kikuchi searches for words to express his feelings, the solemn tone of his voice reflecting the incredulity of that meeting that changed his life. ". . . they are the General Authorities of the entire church!

"President Kimball asked, 'Do you think you can accept this call?' But we couldn't answer because we were too shocked. Finally he asked if we would like to go back to the hotel and talk it over, or perhaps he could leave and let us discuss it in his office.

"Just as he was leaving the room my consciousness returned and I said, 'Please don't leave us alone.'

"He came back smiling and repeated the question: 'Will you accept this call?'

" 'I cannot,' I told him. 'I am not worthy to accept such a calling. I don't mean that I have any problems with moral issues, and I try to live up to the covenants I have made in the holy priesthood and in the House of the Lord and with the responsibilities I have. But I am unworthy to be a General Authority.'

" 'I can understand that,' President Kimball said. 'I have

been through the same thing myself. But the *Lord* has called you.'

"I told him, 'Although I am not capable of this calling as a General Authority, I honor and love the Lord and accept his call. But I want you to know that I am not capable to serve.'

" 'You can do it,' he said. 'You cannot be Spencer, you cannot be Gordon, you cannot be Tom. Just be yourself.' "

Addressing the congregation at general conference later that same day, Elder Kikuchi said, "I am still asking myself and the Lord, 'Why me, O Lord? Why me, O Lord?' Yet, my brothers and sisters, still within my soul I hear . . . , 'I will go where you want me to go, dear Lord.' "

"And so here I am," says Elder Kikuchi today, several years later, with a laugh of wonder and relief. "Even still, I feel I am unworthy of this calling. I have been a member of the First Quorum of the Seventy for many years, but when I go into that special room with the prophet and his counselors and the Quorum of the Twelve and all the other men of God, I pinch myself and say I don't know why I'm here. But I know that this is not man's work — it is the Lord's work. I can serve the Lord in a small way, and any responsibilities I might receive, I want to do with all of my heart and with my deepest commitment."

His responsibilities, like any he has ever held, have also received total dedication and commitment from the Kikuchi family, though it has meant a number of difficult adjustments. Selling all of his business interests and extricating himself from future involvement, he threw himself wholeheartedly into full-time Church service. His first assignment, as executive administrator for Japan and Korea, allowed the family to remain in Tokyo for four years. A complete change of setting was not long off, as his next assignment was managing director of the Church Temple Department, a position he held for five years. During that time he also served as executive administrator of the Murray Granger Area in the Salt Lake Valley for two years and then as a counselor in the Utah North Area presidency for three years.

Moving to Utah was daunting for his wife and children, none of whom spoke English. Coming into a culture that was completely different in traditions and expectations from the one they had left often resulted in feelings of confusion and homesickness. But having the gospel in common with their ward members and many associates, friends, and neighbors, the Kikuchis found themselves welcomed with open arms and eventually began to feel comfortable in their new surroundings.

An illustration of the difficulty of transition—and also their ability to adjust well to a new situation—came when Elder Kikuchi's assignment changed again, this time as president of the Honolulu Hawaii Mission. In their final sacrament meeting in their ward in Bountiful, Utah, Ruka, the Kikuchis' youngest daughter, said, "I lost my friends when I left Japan and came to America, and I am losing them again to go to Hawaii. But wherever the Lord calls my parents, I want to go and be with them because I love the Lord, too."

"I am grateful for the support of my children," affirms Elder Kikuchi. Although they missed their friends in Utah, his family soon felt at home in Hawaii because of the similarities they found to their native Japan. But another move was in the horizon for the Kikuchis, for they were transferred back to Salt Lake City in July 1989. This time they brought only Ruka and their son, Matthew, with them. Their oldest daughter, Sarah, is married and living with her family in Japan, and daughter Rina remained in Hawaii to attend school at Brigham Young University–Hawaii.

Elder Kikuchi enjoys (when he can find the time) carpentry, gardening, and oil painting, both scenery and portraits. He also enjoys reading, especially history, in both English and Japanese. He recently compiled, edited, and published *Proclaiming the Gospel,* a collection of statements by President Spencer W. Kimball on missionary themes. Indeed, President Kimball has always held a very special spot in Elder Kikuchi's heart. He often tells of the time when he saw the prophet, during a visit to Japan, sit on a metal folding chair so the stake presidency could sit on padded chairs. "I felt then what the disciples must have felt when Jesus washed their feet," he says.

Elder Kikuchi later recalled two other incidents: "When I was made stake president I got an envelope – not the Church letterhead but just SWK in the corner. In it the prophet said, 'I just found out you were made stake president. Why didn't you tell me?' And when my brother-in-law was sick, I sent his name to the temple. In a few days, here comes another envelope, SWK. He says, 'The temple president just told me yesterday that your brother-in-law is very ill. I'm so very sorry. I am praying for him.' "

Like his mentor, Elder Kikuchi spreads the gospel with gratitude and as a joyous witness of Christ. His message is simple: "God is our Holy Father; Jesus is our Savior. As we embrace this glorious gospel we may be able to sing the songs of redeeming love. With all the power and faculties of my being, it is my sincere testimony that this is the way of life."

DEREK A. CUTHBERT

"As an eleven-year-old boy I enjoyed the excitement of 1937, the Coronation Year of King George VI and Queen Elizabeth," writes Elder Derek A. Cuthbert. "The event was like a beacon, shining out in a world where war clouds were gathering. Little did I know, as a young boy, that another light was also shining, the light of the restored gospel." (*The Second Century: Latter-day Saints in Great Britain,* Cambridge University Press, 1987, p. 1.)

As young Derek joined in his country's festivities, he was unaware of a quieter, yet perhaps even more significant, celebration that was also taking place: the commemoration of one hundred years of The Church of Jesus Christ of Latter-day Saints in the British Isles. The numbers of British Church members observing this centennial anniversary were few compared to the almost one hundred thousand members who had emigrated to the United States since the first missionaries went to England in 1837. But the next few decades would see a mighty change, for this lad's heart—as well as the hearts of tens of thousands of his countrymen—was being carefully prepared for the illuminating rays of the gospel.

Though the encroaching World War II would leave a beleaguered, weakened Britain, multitudes would subsequently embrace the gospel. Church leaders would no longer urge new converts to gather the Wasatch Mountains of Utah, exhorting them instead to remain in their homeland to fortify "Zion" there. In the centennial year of 1937, the British Mission had approximately 6,000 members in sixty-seven branches and fourteen districts. By the end of the next half-century, there would be 140,000 members in almost four hundred wards and branches, forty stakes, and eight missions. "Because so many had emigrated to America, we were really starting all over. There was that missionary zeal and newness," Elder Cuthbert explained.

Keeping up with such brisk growth would require many leaders, leaders who would come up through the ranks of their own countrymen, leaders like Derek Alfred Cuthbert. Indeed, the name Cuthbert itself was taken by Derek's ancestors many generations earlier in honor of Saint Cuthbert, a seventh-century Christian missionary in England and Scotland. His mother's maiden name, Freck, came from the Anglo-Saxon *fricca*, meaning "preacher." Perhaps the two names were a harbinger of what, or rather who, was to come—a missionary preacher.

Derek's father, Harry Cuthbert, was born in Nottingham, England, and left school at the age of twelve and went to work as an office boy for the *Nottingham Post/Guardian*. After military service in World War I, he returned to the newspaper and remained for fifty years, eventually becoming the publishing manager. In 1920 he married Hilda May Freck, the ninth child of a local baker who had died six months after her birth. The couple settled in the village of Sherwood, named for the nearby Sherwood Forest—fabled hideout of Robin Hood—and had two sons, Norman and Derek Alfred, who was born October 5, 1926.

Harry and Hilda Cuthbert belonged to the Church of England. Although Harry ceased all church activity as an adult, Hilda was a devout member and took her sons to church and taught them to pray and read the Bible. Derek sang in the church choir, establishing the foundation for a lifelong love of music, and drew strength from his study of Bible stories and his mother's strong Christian attitudes. "When you have a prompting to do something good, act upon it straightway," Hilda would tell her sons. Though they struggled through the depression of the 1930s and the years that followed, the Cuthberts encouraged their sons to make the most of each day and seize every opportunity to get an education. Derek became a serious student and was awarded a scholarship to an excellent private institution, Nottingham High School, which the family would not have been able to afford and which would also increase his chances of getting into a good university.

Derek was confirmed into the Church of England in 1938 at the age of twelve. On that day an eleven-year-old girl whom he had previously met, Muriel Olive Mason, was also confirmed. As if renewing a previous relationship, the two fell into an immediate, earnest friendship. To this day Derek cherishes a small diary that Muriel gave him that Christmas (though the chocolates he gave her didn't last nearly so long). They would eventually become sweethearts and would be married in the same church where they were confirmed.

As a boy Derek was active and sociable, playing rugby ("American football without the padding," he laughingly calls it) and cricket and helping to start a bicycle racing club. In high school he won a trophy for his accomplishments in the field sports of javelin, discus, long jump, high jump, and mile and half-mile races.

Childhood was a full, happy time for the Cuthbert boys, who were as close as brothers four years apart in age could be. Then in 1938, a year in which clouds of war were gathering in Europe, their mother had to be hospitalized with a nervous breakdown. Hilda Cuthbert had been very close to her own mother, who had died three years before, and never got over the shock of her death, which Derek felt was a contributing factor in her breakdown. During the rest of her life, though she lived to be eighty-seven, Hilda was in and out of hospitals and never fully recovered. Her illness was a blow for Harry and his two sons, who had to learn to look after themselves. Looking back many years later, Derek felt that his mother's illness had a greater personal effect on his early teenage years than did World War II, and forced him to become more independent and mature.

When Derek was thirteen, England went to war, and though Nottingham was never heavily bombed, he got used to cycling to high school with the air raid sirens screaming overhead. The following year he joined the officer training corps and, at age sixteen, the Home Guard. The next several years were filled with air raid drills and preparation for teenagers, in the absence of older males, to defend England against invasion. Food rationing had already begun before war broke out, and the Cuthberts had learned to live thriftily. Now with war a reality, commodities became even more scarce, with some things not available at all. The basic one-week food rations for one person could fit on a single dinner plate. The Cuthberts supplemented their meager rations with home-grown produce when possible, encouraged by "Dig for Victory," the national campaign for planting gardens. Today Elder Cuthbert, though not able to have a garden, heartily supports the Church's counsel for members to plant gardens wherever possible.

In 1944, toward the end of his last year in high school, Derek joined the Royal Air Force. The duty assignment he preferred was overcrowded, so he was given the option of transferring to the army, working in a coal mine to replace a miner who had gone to war, or taking a language course offered by the Air Ministry in London. Ever since he had begun collecting stamps as a child ("each stamp has a bit of language on it," he explains), he had been fascinated with languages, so he opted for the language course. After basic training in Scotland, he was sent to London University for a crash course in Japanese phonetics, where he was trained to intercept Japanese air-to-ground communications.

In May 1945 two significant events took place: the Allied Forces declared victory in Europe, and Derek and Muriel were married. Two weeks later, Sergeant Cuthbert was sent to the Far East, where war was still raging. The newlyweds, like many other wartime couples, were forced to part, not knowing if they would ever see each other again. While Derek served in Burma, India, and Hong Kong, Muriel lived with her parents, worked in an office, and saved for their future home. She also wrote to her husband at least once a day for a year and a half. At one point he was not able to receive mail, and when it did catch up with him, there were sixty-three letters from his bride. Their letters to each other, though containing a wistful yearning, were not missives of loneliness or despair. Rather, they were full of tender love, feelings of wonder and gratitude for each other, and dreams and plans for the future. "In looking back at that time, it was clear that Muriel and I were meant to be members of the Church and to be together," Elder Cuthbert reflects now. Even though the Church of England does not teach eternal marriage, he adds, "we signed all our letters 'eternally yours.' "

After he returned to England, Sergeant Cuthbert worked in the Air Ministry in London, tracking down information on servicemen who were reported missing in action in the German theater of war. Though it was "good preparation for later genealogical research," he says, it was a sad assignment. But the best part of the situation was that he was able to travel home to Nottingham every weekend to be with Muriel.

January 1948 was a big month for the Cuthberts: Derek was released from the service, he started studying at the University of Nottingham on a government grant for servicemen, and their first child, Janis, was born. Because Derek had diligently studied for his college courses during his military tenure, he was able to skip the first year of his university studies, and he graduated with honors in economics and law two and a half years later. His interest in athletics also led him to qualify as an amateur coach and to represent the university in javelin throwing.

In the summer of 1950, Derek began working as a management trainee for British Celanese Limited. Eventually he became an expert on petroleum chemical economics and worked his way up to financial manager of a factory with more than ten thousand employees.

These early years were also a period of growth and change for the Cuthberts, who moved into a new house; had their second daughter, Maureen; and were active in their church. They were not searching for anything new, particularly a new religion. In fact, they knew virtually nothing about the restored church except that Muriel knew that a great-uncle and his family had become "Mormons" and had emigrated to Wyoming in the 1880s, and that a distant "Mormon" cousin was serving a mission somewhere in England. She didn't know what a "Mormon" was, but was vaguely interested to know what they believed. (Later, after they had joined the

Church, they also learned that Muriel's grandmother and great-grandmother had also been baptized.)

That August missionaries were knocking on doors in the Cuthberts' neighborhood. Discouraged by the lack of response, they were about to leave the area when one of them said, "No, let's just try one last door, and then we will close this area." That "one last door" turned out to be the Cuthberts'. Muriel answered their knock and, recognizing them as Mormons, asked if they knew her cousin. They said they knew of him, and then they asked the only question that probably could have caught her attention, "Could you believe that there is a prophet on the earth today?"

This was the same question Muriel had asked her minister when she was twelve. She had never been satisfied by his answer: "No, we don't need one. The Bible is sufficient." At her invitation, the young men returned later, when Derek was home.

The Cuthberts were impressed with the sincerity of the young men, and when the missionaries showed Derek a card illustrated with a reproduction of some Egyptian hieroglyphics that Joseph Smith had copied from ancient records, he received a witness that the Book of Mormon was true — before he had even studied it. The missionaries also taught the family to pray together. Derek and Muriel readily accepted all of the principles and doctrines of the Church except one: tithing. "It is not possible," Derek commented when the elders first introduced the principle. "We are really struggling to get by, doing our accounts by half-pennies. We cannot pay tithing."

"Everyone can pay tithing," was the reply. "It is the first item of expense."

Later Elder Cuthbert said, "That wise answer has been a great strength to me and to the many others that I have shared it with. And sure enough, we found that when we paid one-tenth to the Lord before anything else, he helped us use the other nine-tenths more effectively."

After investigating The Church of Jesus Christ of Latter-day Saints for five months, Derek believed it was true, but he didn't feel the need to actually be baptized and leave the church his family had belonged to for generations. A discussion on the need for priesthood authority finally changed his mind, though he didn't make his decision known immediately.

One evening in January 1951, just as the missionaries were leaving, one of them asked, "Brother and Sister Cuthbert, is there anything we can do for you before we leave?"

"Well, there is one thing," Derek replied. "My wife and I would like to be baptized."

Muriel gazed at her husband in amazement. Although he knew that she was ready for baptism, she didn't realize that he was ready also. The missionaries promised to make arrangements for the baptism to take place the coming Saturday and then left abruptly. Several years later the Cuthberts found out why they had departed so quickly. Apparently all of the missionaries in the district had been fasting and praying that day for the Cuthberts, and the two elders had gone outside to kneel down on a little patch of grass and offer a prayer of thanksgiving.

On a cold wintry evening, January 27, 1951, Muriel and Derek were baptized in a blue-tiled font recently constructed by the missionaries. Their baptism changed forever the shape, pattern, and outlook of their lives. They were shunned by many of their friends—some literally crossing the road to avoid contact with them—and family members, and although most of the rejection gradually softened, none of their extended family ever joined the Church. A friend who had warned Derek that he would never get ahead in business if he didn't smoke or drink consequently went bankrupt, while Derek prospered.

The Nottingham Branch extended open arms of fellowship, and the Cuthberts felt they had come home. Soon after his baptism, Derek was called to the mission board of the Young Men's Mutual Improvement Association and spent most weekends visiting the various districts by train. As the new converts began incorporating the gospel into their lives, they discovered another financial strain, in addition to tithing: they didn't own a car, and it took an additional ten percent of their income for transportation to and from meetings. But, although many felt it premature for the junior trainee, Derek received his first promotion in his company soon after he joined the Church. Money was still very tight, but their income had increased to cover the new expenses.

Being Latter-day Saints in England in the 1950s presented many problems: there wasn't a vehicle or a telephone in the whole Nottingham Branch and communication was difficult; there was a paucity of local leadership; and the branches all met in run-down rented facilities, and many new buildings were needed. Although the war had been over for five years, some foods were still rationed, and economic conditions were difficult for the entire country. Elder Spencer W. Kimball, then a member of the Council of the Twelve, toured the British Mission in 1955 with a message to the Saints: "Stay and build the Church." Though many members still sought greener pastures in the United States, the Cuthberts decided right from the start to stay where they were and help build the Church in England.

Derek was ordained an elder within nine months of his conversion and was rapidly drawn into leadership positions, serving as branch and district president, counselor to four mission presidents, and stake president, and in June 1970, he was called to serve as regional representative for the whole

British Isles. Most weekends were spent away on assignment as he saw to the needs of a growing Church membership and an ambitious program of chapel construction.

The Cuthberts had always wanted children, Muriel often saying she hoped to have four boys. But in the light of their new understanding of families in the Lord's plan, their desires broadened and they eventually had ten children. "My wife often says that we got our four boys — with a bonus of six girls," Elder Cuthbert remarked. They had resolved never to leave their children alone, and if one of the parents had to be away, the other would stay at home. Though Derek was often away, many evenings it was he who bathed the children and put them to bed as Muriel attended to her Church responsibilities. She held positions in Relief Society and the Young Women's Mutual Improvement Association for many years, and was often involved in writing pantomimes, skits, and roadshows.

The Cuthberts eagerly awaited the time they could be sealed for eternity, and in 1955 they attended joyously the groundbreaking of the London Temple at Newchapel, some 150 miles from Nottingham. When the Swiss Temple was dedicated that same year, Derek felt a strong desire to be present at the dedicatory services. Though they couldn't afford for them both to make the fifteen-hundred-mile round-trip, their meager savings gave them the equivalent of about one hundred dollars, just enough to purchase one train ticket. Muriel packed enough food to last the two and a half days Derek would be gone. Being present and hearing the inspiring words of President David O. McKay was the crowning spiritual experience of his life to that point. He came home rededicated to preparing his family to go to the temple together as soon as possible.

Three years later President McKay returned to dedicate the London Temple. Following the ceremonies, Derek and

Muriel — eight months pregnant — and their five children, ages two to ten, were the first family to be sealed on the day the temple officially opened.

For sixteen months in 1961 and 1962, Derek took leave from his job in order to help establish Deseret Enterprises, an organization that would function as a commercial source of supplies for the expanding Church in Great Britain and the Commonwealth. Later, when the new business was running smoothly, his company took him back, although it was normally against their policy to do so. During the same time he also served as the business manager for the *Millennial Star*, the official Church publication for the British Isles, which was printed from 1840 through 1970.

For Derek and Muriel Cuthbert, the 1960s and 1970s were filled with growth and development. As their children matured and one by one left home for schooling, work, or marriage, they were grateful that they had joined the Church early in their marriage and that their children had grown up as members. Janis, the eldest and first to leave, went to BYU in 1965 and was soon engaged. They knew there was no way they could afford for both of them to travel to her wedding, but they felt that at least one of them should attend. So Derek sold his collection of Church books and used the proceeds to buy Muriel a plane ticket to the United States. Later, he was able buy the books back and eventually to amass a library of more than a thousand volumes.

A significant event to Elder Cuthbert, as well as to the Church in Britain, came in 1968 when Elder Kimball returned to England to form the Birmingham Stake. On the day after stake conference, Elder and Sister Kimball met with local leaders and missionaries atop Herefordshire Beacon, a knoll in the Malvern Hills that was a significant historic site in early Church history. Just before the meeting, a misty rain began to fall. "Of course, when you go to meet the Lord in a mountain, you can expect there to be a cloud," Elder Kimball commented.

One of the men lent his coat to Elder Kimball to keep him dry, while the others assembled shivered in the chilly morning air. But as he spoke, Elder Cuthbert recalled, "we were enveloped by a warm, tangible spirit and were quite comfortable. It was one of the most spiritual events in my life." Later, Elder Kimball declared of the surrounding area, "This is the place where the blood of Israel is richly concentrated and there are many still to gather."

"It was a time of rededication . . . throughout Britain," Elder Cuthbert wrote later. "Many times in the years that followed, President Kimball would ask Sister Cuthbert and me: 'Do you remember that wonderful day on the Malvern Hills?' " (*The Second Century*, p. 87.)

Another significant event was the area conference held in Manchester, England, in August 1971, the first such conference of the Church in this century. There was a sense of history in the making as Elder Cuthbert, then the regional representative of the Twelve for the six regions in the British Isles, was directed by the First Presidency to oversee the preparations. This conference, he was told, would be the prototype for future conferences held around the world. In an atmosphere of rejoicing and excitement, the British Saints prepared for the conference for ten months. The conference would be attended by President Joseph Fielding Smith and thirteen other Brethren, the largest representation of General Authorities ever assembled outside the United States.

When Jessie Evans Smith, beloved wife of the prophet, died just days before the conference, the British Saints prayed that President Smith would still come to Manchester. He did, and the twelve thousand persons who gathered for the conference received his blessing as he told them that the Church was coming of age in Great Britain and was being built up and strengthened there among some of the best people on earth. "How grateful we were for a prophet in our land!" Elder Cuthbert declared. The enthusiastic spirit of missionary revival lingered on in Great Britain long after the meetings were over.

Elder Cuthbert was asked to chauffeur President Smith during part of his stay in England, an assignment he accepted with delight. A picture taken of the two leaders in an English rose garden appeared on the cover of the November 1971 *Ensign* and hangs framed on Elder Cuthbert's office wall, a cherished reminder of three unforgettable days spent with a prophet of the Lord.

Ever since they joined the Church, Derek and Muriel had planned to serve a mission, assuming it would be when he retired in 1990. They were surprised and pleased, however, when he was called to preside over the Scotland Edinburgh Mission in 1975. They sold their home to help finance their mission and moved to Scotland with seven of their children. The years spent in full-time missionary service were happy ones for the family. "We saw it as a way of repaying our Father in heaven for the missionaries who traveled six thousand miles to knock on our door," explains Elder Cuthbert.

When President Cuthbert recognized the lack of priesthood leadership as one of the mission's weaknesses, he determined to do something about it. In 1840 Elder Orson Pratt of the Council of the Twelve visited Arthur's Seat, the highest point in Edinburgh, and petitioned the Lord for two hundred converts; within a few months, more than this number were baptized. On a snowy New Year's day in 1976, Elder and Sister Cuthbert, with their children and a few missionaries, ascended the same hill, now known to the Saints as Pratt's Hill, and there a special prayer was offered for three hundred men to be raised up in Scotland to provide leadership for the Church in Scotland. During the time Elder Cuthbert served as mission president, almost exactly that many men, with their families, joined the Church in the mission.

One afternoon in March 1978, just three months before the end of his mission, President Cuthbert received a phone call from President Kimball. After ascertaining that Sister Cuthbert was also on the line, the prophet extended a call to President Cuthbert to become a a member of the First Quorum of the Seventy.

The Cuthberts had mixed emotions concerning the unexpected calling — feelings of joy, wonder, and inadequacy, mingled with sadness at leaving their beloved England. After having pledged to "stay and build up the Church" in England, and urging other converts to do the same, they felt sad as they departed at the end of their three-year mission term and immigrated to the United States. Though they would return on visits and extended assignments, Salt Lake City would be their home base. Adjusting to a new culture and new traditions wasn't too difficult for the Cuthberts, though Elder Cuthbert does admit, with tongue in cheek, that his children had a bit of difficulty with the new language. "I think it was Churchill who said, 'Great Britain and the United States: two great nations separated by a common language!' " he quips.

Elder Cuthbert's first assignment as a General Authority was area supervisor for Idaho, where he received experience in meeting the needs of a concentrated Church membership and learned about welfare farms and production. Three years later he was delighted when he was called to be executive administrator of the British Isles/Africa Area. He was able to take his family to Solihull, England, for the first year of this assignment; then he administered the area for two more years by commuting from Salt Lake City. Subsequent assignments have taken him and Sister Cuthbert to various parts of the United States, Canada, Europe, Africa, and South America, including a year in Quito, Ecuador, and six months in Frankfurt, Germany.

Elder Cuthbert's military experiences in the Far East, coupled with his Church service in Africa and South America, have given him special empathy for the problems and needs of peoples in Third World countries. "More than half of the people in the world live in countries where the per capita income is less than three hundred dollars—not per week or per month, but per *year*," he says. "In some countries in Africa, it is less than one hundred dollars per year. We must reorient ourselves to become a Zion society with one heart and one mind and no poor among us."

He is also keenly aware of the challenges involved in taking the gospel to such countries. While acknowledging that the most important thing the Church can take to anyone is the gospel, he feels that the Saints also need to render Christian service. When people from impoverished nations join the Church, what they need is not a handout, he explains, but help in helping themselves. He was in Ghana, West Africa, during the drought of 1983, and observed that the Saints there were lucky if they had one meal a day. A memorable experience came in a training meeting for new district presidencies in Nigeria in 1981. After Elder Cuthbert and the mission president had presented their messages and instructions, many hands went up with questions. One new leader asked if the Church could provide the people with certain basic items, reading a list from a pad in his hand. Before Elder Cuthbert could respond, another Nigerian leader got up, walked to the front of the room, faced the group, and said, "The Church? Can the Church provide? Brethren, *we* are the Church."

At the same time Elder Cuthbert speaks of privations and hardships, his words are also filled with glowing praise for the spirituality of the members in Africa, South America, and other impoverished countries, and of their joy, humility, and readiness to embrace the gospel.

He has always had great interest in peoples and languages of the world. His personal library contains scriptures, grammars, and readers in thirty-seven languages, and he has studied twelve of them and given conference talks in five. Another hobby is Old English illuminated writing, which he often uses to inscribe cards, certificates, and other gifts for friends and family members.

Christmas 1989 brought a joyful, yet somber, reunion to the Cuthbert clan — which included sons and daughters, sons-in-law and daughters-in-law, and grandchildren. Because their oldest child, Janis, had married and settled in America before their last three children were born, the Cuthberts had previously had all of their children together only once, when Janis and her family went to England for a visit. This Christmas gathering was accompanied by a special urgency, for the family members knew it might be the last time they would see their father and grandfather on this earth.

For most of his life Elder Cuthbert's physical condition had always been robust and hardy. Then in 1976, repeated falls and a lack of sensation in his feet and legs led to a diagnosis of peripheral neuropathy, a condition that could be neither treated nor cured. Yet other than some lameness and the need to use leg braces, the condition didn't slow him down much. He also later developed diabetes and altitude sickness. Then in January 1989, he came down with a severe case of bronchitis, which worsened despite antibiotics and other medications. By midyear, though he was keeping up with an arduous schedule of stake conference visits, he felt exhausted after each assignment. In October, he again sought medical care for his continually declining condition. After a battery of tests, he was told he had cancer in its last stages and it had diffused through both lungs. Cancer. The word rang ominously through his mind. Had he not sought medical help when he did, he could have died within two weeks, the specialist told him.

Elder Cuthbert was put on oxygen immediately, and surgery was scheduled for October 31—"Halloween," he points out, a wry smile on his lips, his sense of humor as healthy as ever. "The nurses were all dressed in strange costumes, and some had red or green hair. I said, 'If the doctors are dressed as Dracula, I'm going home.' " Following the surgery, he began a program of chemotherapy. Though the treatment often caused fatigue and mood swings, as therapy continued his lung capacity returned to normal and repeated studies showed a marked improvement in his condition. In February 1990, results of tests were within normal limits, and there was little evidence of the disease left in his body.

As Church members learned of his condition, Elder Cuthbert experienced an outpouring of love and encouragement through cards, letters, and phone calls from all over the world. He credits his restored health to these, along with many fasts and with priesthood blessings from his Brethren and from sons and sons-in-law. "May I express my love and gratitude for the prayers and blessings and loving concern on my behalf which have brought about a miracle of recovery," he told the congregation at the next general conference. "As I give thanks for each new day of life, I express gratitude for the opportunities of service—past, present and future." (*Ensign*, May 1990, p. 13.)

As a child Elder Cuthbert sang the Psalms each Sunday with the choir in his Church of England congregation. Over the years he developed a special love for that section of the Bible. With Christmas 1989 approaching, he spent a lot of time in prayer and scripture reading, focusing particularly on the Psalms. On Christmas Day, though very ill, he wrote his own psalm, a hymn of gratitude and praise to our Father in

Heaven. He dedicated this hymn of praise to all whose loving concern contributed to this special time in his life:

My soul delighteth in the Lord, my God;
He hath answered the petition of many:
In Him do I put my trust forever,
For He hath fulfilled his promise toward me.

Lift up your heads, ye troubled and weary;
Open your hearts who are lonely and in need:
The Lord, who giveth peace, shall comfort you;
He will bind up the hurt and lighten the load.

Let us magnify the Lord together
And sing of the wonder of His sacred birth;
For He hath brought salvation and mercy;
He hath broken the bands of darkness and death.

He hath opened the windows of heaven;
He hath blessed the faithful for all their good works.
Great is the Lord, and worthy of our praises;
The Kingdom of God He hath established.

The mountain of the Lord's House hath He builded,
In glory, in the tops of the mountains;
The fulness of the gospel hath He restored
In latter days, as anciently foretold.

Blessed be the Lord God of Israel;
He hath done a marvelous work and a wonder.
The Lord shall reign in honour and glory;
May we be ready to receive Him gladly.

TED E. BREWERTON

Elder Ted E. Brewerton could hardly contain his excitement as he carefully turned the yellowed pages of the tattered booklet. For more than ten years he had searched for this treasure in secondhand bookstores and libraries in North and South America. The ragged cover bore the inscription *The Title of the Lords of Totonicapan*, printed in elaborate block letters. As he reverently leafed through the rare edition, his eyes feasted on the Old Spanish text and came to rest on the final page, which bore the signatures of the Lords of Totonicapan. Fifteen scrawled symbols, belonging to the ancient American tribal chieftains, certified, with their honor and by their own words, that this was indeed an accurate record of the ancient oral history and legends of their peoples.

Recorded in 1554 in the city of Totonicapan, in what is now Guatemala, this was one of the few existing accounts of oral Mayan legends handed down through the Quiche Indians, descendants of the Mayans. Some 280 years later, in 1834, these legends were translated from the Indian dialect into Spanish and verified by their courts. But it was not until 1885 – 331 years after the initial transcribing of the accounts – that a few copies of the booklet were finally printed in France.

For more than twenty years Elder Brewerton had studied the records of the first historians who had come to the New World with the Spanish conquerors in the sixteenth century. He was determined to obtain his own copy of *The Title of the Lords of Totonicapan,* but he was told that the only extant copies were tightly controlled in a few European museums and libraries and that his search would undoubtedly prove fruitless. However, his perseverance finally paid off, for in 1967 he discovered and purchased a copy in a small bookstore in the Virgin Islands.

At the time Elder Brewerton was serving as a mission president in Central America, and as he read the account, a thrill of comprehension ran through him. The basic themes of the writings – that the people spoken of in the record knew themselves to be children of Israel, descendants of Abraham and with the same language and customs, and that their forefathers had come from across the sea, from Babylonia – dovetailed perfectly with gospel teachings and the Book of Mormon account of the peopling of ancient America.

In 1985 Elder Brewerton, by then a member of the First Quorum of the Seventy and in the presidency of the Mexico/ Central America Area, learned that the original text of the booklet he prized so highly was not available for study outside Europe. It had been rewritten in modern Spanish, and it was that version that was being studied in schools in Central America. He also realized what the original text could mean to the people of present-day Totonicapan, Guatemala, and the other countries of the region.

During a visit to Guatemala, Elder Brewerton traveled to Totonicapan, where he visited the main civic library. "Are you familiar with *The Title of the Lords of Totonicapan?*" he asked the head librarian.

"Of course, it is our book," he was told. "Why do you ask?"

"Do you have the original text?"

"No, *no está en casa*—it is not home where it belongs," was the librarian's reply.

When Elder Brewerton told the librarian that he had an original copy of the booklet and was willing to give Totonicapan an authentic bound copy, printed on fine bond paper with an embossed cover and each page notarized, the librarian was incredulous. "It would be the best thing that ever happened to this city," he said. But, he added, the mayor would want the presentation to be done right—ceremoniously in the national theater on a live radio broadcast, with government and education officials present.

Elder Brewerton then told him of another book he possessed that was also an ancient document that coincided with *The Title of the Lords of Totonicapan,* a book that also spoke of the origins of the early Americans and the coming of Christ to the Americas—the Book of Mormon.

"Could you also present that book to the mayor?" the librarian asked.

"I believe I could arrange that," Elder Brewerton responded with characteristic understatement, the shadow of a smile on his face.

Eventually, Elder Brewerton presented certified, bound copies of *The Title of the Lords of Totonicapan* to the heads of the national museums and libraries of Guatemala and Mexico. Upon receipt of the gift, the University of Mexico in Mexico City immediately undertook a detailed study of the text. In return for these gifts, the Church has gained access to many old documents and records for microfilming, and a few long-closed doors have been opened to the gospel. Elder Brewerton kept one of the authenticated copies and donated his original booklet to the J. Reuben Clark Law Library at Brigham Young University, which has been designated as the western United States repository for ancient American documents. The booklet has since been translated into English and printed by the University of Oklahoma Press.

The opportunity to return these ancient Mayan legends to the people has been just one high point in Elder Brewerton's lifelong love of Latin American history and peoples. It is an interest that began when he was called to serve a mission in Uruguay in 1949, and has continued through the years as he and Sister Brewerton—and at times some or all of their six children—have lived in Uruguay, Paraguay, Chile, Costa Rica, Brazil, Mexico, and Argentina. In 1965 Elder Brewerton was called as president of the Costa Rica San Jose Mission. Since his call to the First Quorum of the Seventy in 1978, his assignments have been primarily to Central and South America, including presiding over the Church in Brazil, in the Mexico North Area, and in Argentina. He has also served as a member of the presidency of the North America West Area.

However, even more notable than his enthusiasm for Latin America is his love of the gospel and his appreciation for his heritage: a legacy of Church membership. He is a fourth-generation Mormon: his four great-grandfathers were among the Church's earliest converts in England and Scotland and emigrated to the United States, traveling westward with the Saints. His ancestors were among the first settlers in Payson and Meadow, Utah; one great-grandfather, Charles Brewerton, served as Payson's mayor and was a popular speaker in sacrament meetings and funerals. Both the Brewertons and the Fishers (his mother's parents) moved to Alberta, Canada, just after the turn of the century and helped colonize the small town of Raymond, one of the thirteen fledgling Mormon settlements in southern Alberta.

Lee Brewerton, Elder Brewerton's father, was nine years old in 1903 when his family moved to Canada. That same year his future companion, Jane Fisher, was born in Utah, and just seven days later her mother took her north to join her father, who had already moved to Raymond. Lee and Jane grew up — as do most residents of small towns — knowing each other's families well, though they were not close themselves because of the difference in their ages. That difference mattered not at all as they matured and fell in love. After their marriage, Lee opened a chain of movie theaters in partnership with his brothers, and Lee and Jane Brewerton established themselves as a family dedicated to church and community service.

The Brewertons were blessed with two sons, born two years apart. The youngest, born March 30, 1925, was Teddy Eugene. Ted flourished in the wholesome, small-town atmosphere, a perfect setting for an active, growing child. The educational system, among the best in Canada, offered students opportunities to participate in a wide variety of educational and extracurricular activities, and Teddy excelled in athletics as well as academics. He was involved in boxing and track and was on the first string of the high school basketball team, a team that took the provincewide championship, playing against high schools in Alberta cities that were much bigger than Raymond.

The Brewertons were a loving, active family who worked together in the movie theaters and in their yard and garden, and played together on the golf course and badminton court. Through example and precept, Lee and Jane instilled in their sons the virtues of honesty, hard work, and service. Even as a very young boy, Ted enjoyed working alongside his father cleaning the big theaters. He eventually experienced every area of the business, from selling concessions and tickets to whatever else was needed.

Looking back on his childhood, Elder Brewerton believes that one of his major advantages was the high-caliber example of the people he associated with both in church and in school. Many years later when as a General Authority he returned to a stake conference in Raymond, he was humbled to look out over the congregation and say to himself, "These people can do anything; they are highly educated and have a total devotion to the Church. Why am I the one standing here?"

World War II was in full swing when Ted turned eighteen and enlisted in the Royal Canadian Air Force. Being plunged into military life in eastern Canada was an abrupt change for the rural Mormon boy. As he became aware of the many different life-styles and conditions outside his early experiences, he came to appreciate his solid upbringing even more, and his childhood faith matured into a resolute foundation. He started training as a single-engine fighter pilot, but when the war began to taper off, he was transferred into the Canadian army, where he received advanced training as an infantry signaler. He was scheduled to be sent to the Pacific Theater when the war ended, without his ever leaving Canada or seeing combat.

Because of his excellent record of training and volunteerism, Ted was promptly discharged in order to attend the University of Alberta in Edmonton, receiving twenty months of tuition and a living stipend as compensation for his twenty months of military service. When the twenty months was up, his grades were good enough that the government continued to finance his education, and he completed a bachelor of science in pharmacology.

Though Ted was offered a well-paying job when he graduated at age twenty-four, he felt a strong desire to serve a mission, an important goal that had already been put off too long. He was interviewed for his mission by Joseph Fielding Smith, then serving as a member of the Council of the Twelve. At the conclusion of the interview he asked Elder Smith if he might suggest where he would like to serve.

"We don't generally do that, but go ahead," said Elder Smith.

Ted said he wanted to go to either Palestine or South America. Even so, when he received his mission call, he was surprised to be called to Uruguay. He spoke no Spanish and only a little French, and had never heard of a Canadian being called to a mission in South America.

When Marion G. Romney, then an Assistant to the Council of the Twelve, set Ted apart for his mission, he gave the young elder a blessing that would influence him for the rest of his life. Two things in particular stood out. First, Elder Romney promised him, "You will preach the gospel without even speaking. They will know the truth because of your eyes." This was borne out on several occasions; once, in particular, he received a letter from a new convert who told him, "Even before you started to speak, I knew the Church was true because I saw it in your eyes."

The second remarkable counsel in his blessing affected Elder Brewerton so greatly that many years later he would refer to Elder Romney as the "most influential teacher in my life." Elder Romney told him to study the gospel with a system—to select a topic and study that subject in depth in the scriptures and in other appropriate Church sources. Though Elder Brewerton had not studied the gospel this way before, he had used that method successfully at the university, so why not use it with the gospel? He immediately instituted this practice and found that it bore much fruit throughout his mission and after he returned home. As an institute teacher, a bishop, a mission president, a stake president, a regional representative, and a General Authority, he has continued this type of gospel study and has advised others to do the same. Through the years he became known for his depth of understanding of many subjects, and he received hundreds of requests to speak on those topics. He also successfully applied this learning method to his secular interests, including political theories, archaeology, and pharmaceutical chemistry. In a newspaper interview he explained: "If one studies faithfully in this systematic way, he will find that his confidence in the Lord will increase and his feelings of security and happiness within the Church will grow immeasurably." (*Church News*, April 22, 1978, p. 2.)

Elder Brewerton spent almost three years on his mission in Uruguay—the thirty-month term of his call and a three-month extension. His testimony grew and crystallized and he received valuable proselyting and leadership experience, serving as a branch president when he had been out only a few months, as a district president, and even a short term as a Relief Society president in an area with a scarcity of leaders.

Within four days after he returned to Raymond, Ted found a job as a pharmacist. Not long after that, he became acquainted with Dorothy Hall, a pretty eighteen-year-old who was in town visiting her grandmother. Though Dorothy was born in Raymond, her family moved to Vancouver, British Columbia, when she was ten, so she and Ted had not been well-acquainted. Now he was taken with her beauty—she had already won several beauty titles—as well as her happy spirit and dedication to the Lord. After her visit, the two commuted between Vancouver and Raymond to see each other.

After one of his visits to Vancouver, Ted realized that this was the woman he wanted to marry, so when he got home he wrote and proposed. Unaware of the message he had written, Dorothy read his letter aloud to her parents, who were as taken by surprise as she was. Her answer was neither yes nor no, but "later." Within a few months, Ted received another letter accepting his proposal.

Dorothy's father was a convert to the Church and unable to go to the temple as yet, so Ted wrote to President David O. McKay and asked what they should do. President McKay answered that because of this and other circumstances, they could be married in Vancouver by the branch president and then drive to the Alberta Temple to be sealed (a practice that is not allowed today). Thus, Ted and Dorothy were married February 11, 1955, in Vancouver, and six days later they were sealed in the Alberta Temple.

The couple established their new home in Lethbridge, Alberta, where Ted opened a pharmacy and Dorothy found work as an X-ray technician. The next year the couple were very distressed when Dorothy had a miscarriage, but the following year their son David was born, and two years later, a daughter, Michelle. The years in Lethbridge were busy ones for the new pharmacist, who worked up to seventy-two hours a week honing his craft, yet trying to reserve as much time as possible for his family and church service.

The heavy workload proved invaluable in 1959 when an opportunity that "every pharmacist would want but very few are able to get" came to Ted Brewerton. A group of twenty-five physicians were building a large medical complex in Calgary and were looking for an experienced pharmacist to open a dispensary there. Many individuals applied for the position, but after meeting with some of the doctors involved, Ted drove back to Lethbridge and told Dorothy he knew he would be selected. Though he had no real reason to believe that, he would later find out that Calgary was indeed where the Lord wanted the Brewertons to be. A few months later a letter came informing him that the position was his.

The Brewertons sold their business and home in Lethbridge and moved to Calgary, where they purchased a lot on which to build a new home. Soon after the construction was begun, Ted was called to be the bishop of the ward in which his new home was located. Though the pharmacy was expected to lose money for the first year, after ninety days the business was consistently in the black, and within a fairly short time it was the largest pharmacy in Canada, with a large professional staff dispensing several hundred prescriptions daily and amassing the most comprehensive medical library in the province. Ted, who eventually opened a second apothecary in northern Calgary, became widely recognized as a leader in his field and was asked to present papers at conventions and to give a series of lectures and serve on panels.

Perhaps the highlight of his professional career came when he received the Bowl of Hygeia Award. The award, the highest honor that can be conferred upon a pharmacist, is presented to an individual who has rendered outstanding service outside the pharmaceutical profession. His picture and an article about the presentation were featured in *Time* magazine, and he and Dorothy were honored at an awards banquet in Richmond, Virginia. Though his professional accomplishments were touted, most of the comments concerned his many years of religious involvement. Those present were astonished at the amount of time and effort he devoted to the Church—all without pay. After the ceremonies, many lined up to talk to him. "I thought then that this is why I won the award," he reflected later, "because it created such a receptive atmosphere for gospel discussion."

In 1964 Jane Brewerton, Ted's mother, traveled to England in pursuit of a heartfelt love—genealogy. She was gone five months, much longer than originally intended, but returned with more than eight thousand names from her and her husband's lines—enough to keep them both busy completing entry sheets and doing temple work for the rest of their lives. Shortly before she died in 1988, Jane passed the remnants of her research on to her sons. Combing through the boxes and piles has been a huge undertaking for Elder Brewerton, but his mother's hard work is still bearing fruit, for he has been able to submit hundreds of additional names for temple work.

Six years after moving to Calgary, the Brewertons, whose family now included two more daughters, Andrea and Leanne, found themselves in Central America. Ted had been called to serve as president of the new Costa Rica San Jose Mission. The mission's boundaries encompassed Nicaragua, Honduras, Costa Rica, and Panama. A year later Venezuela, which had never before had missionaries, was added to the mission. Elder Marion G. Romney, in his prayer dedicating Venezuela for missionary work, asked that the people would "recognize the Book of Mormon as a true account of their forefathers." Within eighteen months fifty missionaries were serving in that country, and President Brewerton encouraged them to look for potential priesthood bearers who would in turn bring their families into the Church. Proselyting, which went slowly at first, gradually picked up, and today there are two missions in Venezuela.

With a mission spread over such a wide area, President and Sister Brewerton often felt they saw more of the inside of a plane than anything else, for every six weeks they visited the major cities in each of the five countries. Sister Brewerton also became involved in improvising programs and manuals to teach Indians who had no written language. But despite the challenges, the work progressed and the family enjoyed their experience in the mission field.

While he was in Central America, Elder Romney gave a special blessing to Sister Brewerton, who, as a result of a rare blood disorder, had previously suffered two miscarriages (one of which had nearly taken her life) and was now threatening to miscarry again. "We told Elder Romney of our dilemma and he said, 'Let's see what the Lord has in mind,' " recalls

Elder Brewerton. "He put his hands on her head and for a short time he spoke to the Lord as one would to a close friend. Then he literally purged her system of the blood disease."

When Sister Brewerton visited the doctor soon afterward, he could find no trace of the disorder. Six months later she gave birth to a healthy baby girl, Lycia, and three years after that, a healthy baby boy, Michael. "A doctor told us later that the chances of her having a normal delivery, considering the symptoms she had exhibited, was as unusual and unlikely as someone overcoming a progressive state of cancer. He said that he had never heard of anyone with her disorder being completely cured," Elder Brewerton adds.

A highlight of the Brewertons' years in Central America came in September 1965, when Panama's San Blas Islands, home to more than thirty thousand Cuna Indians, were opened to the gospel. The missionaries were invited to a gathering of chieftains on the largest island to tell about the Church. President Brewerton spoke in Spanish about the Book of Mormon, and especially of Christ's visit to the Americas, with his words translated into the Indian dialect. As he finished, a spokesman of the Indians, a dark-skinned man about five feet tall, stood and looked up at the mission president, who was almost a foot taller. "Our God that visited here was white like you, not dark like me," he said. "He was tall like you, not short like me, and he had a beard like you, not beardless like me. He came down out of the heavens and healed the sick and told us to share with each other. He also said that one day he would return. Maybe he was the same as this Jesus you talk about in your book."

The next afternoon President Brewerton explained the same things to the chief who presided over all sixty of the islands. "We don't have a written language, but we have these pictographs which trigger back, as a mnemonic device, an old piece of our history," the chief told him, sketching some symbols on a paper. "This one tells me that we once had our ancient history recorded and it was hidden in this mountain, covered over with jungle. It disappeared with the promise that somehow one day it would be returned to us."

"That is what we are returning to you," said President Brewerton, "the Book of Mormon." The missionaries went on to have much success among the Cuna Indians.

In 1968 the Brewertons returned to Calgary, and over the next few years Elder Brewerton continued to serve the Church: as counselor in a stake presidency, president of the Calgary Alberta Stake, and regional representative.

For many years Ted and Dorothy had eagerly anticipated to an extended vacation to Latin America, and finally it looked as though the trip would come to fruition in late 1978. Then, shortly before that time, each decided independently that the trip should be canceled. Although they had looked forward to the trip with great excitement, for some reason both felt it wasn't the right thing at the time. (A similar experience had occurred in 1962 when they had called off a trip to Europe that would have taken them away during the very week Elder Brewerton was called as a bishop.)

A few days later they learned why. While they were in Salt Lake City attending general conference and a regional representatives' seminar, Elder Brewerton received a call from D. Arthur Haycock asking him to meet with "the President" that same afternoon. Though Ted knew Brother Haycock was secretary to President Spencer W. Kimball, he assumed the meeting was with Ezra Taft Benson, who was then serving as president of the Council of the Twelve and who was in charge of the seminar.

When he arrived for the appointment and saw President Kimball at the end of the hall waiting for him, the truth struck Elder Brewerton like a thunderbolt. President Kimball invited him to sit down and, with few preliminaries, looked him in the eye and said, "You are being called to be a General Authority, a member of the First Quorum of the Seventy." Though Elder Brewerton was speechless, he managed to indicate his acceptance. When President Kimball learned that Sister Brewerton was also in town, he asked Elder Brewerton to go get her, and then the meeting continued with the three of them.

The magnitude of his commitment became apparent a few days later at a meeting of the General Authorities in the Salt Lake Temple. After asking the three new seventies to stand, President Kimball said, "Elder Brewerton, are you aware that you could be called at *any time* to go *anywhere?* Are you willing to do that?"

"Even though I knew I was making a full-time, life-time commitment, it hadn't hit me with quite the force that it did at that moment," said Elder Brewerton. "When you make a promise in the sacred House of the Lord in front of all of those witnesses, how could you not keep it?" Two weeks later he had the chance to begin keeping his pledge when he was called to preside over the Brazil Area.

In 1987, many countries and assignments later, Elder Brewerton was in Paraguay when he heard of a group of Nivaclé Indians who had been converted after one of their number had joined the Church in Asunción. Desiring to teach their children the gospel and be able to live its principles without outside influences, the entire group of 214 persons had moved to a remote, unpopulated area of the country, but heavy floods destroyed their beautiful new meetinghouse, their homes, and all of their belongings. They then moved to a new location, only to lose what little they had left when the floods came again the next year.

A small party, including Elder Brewerton and the mission president, set out in two four-wheel-drive trucks loaded with supplies and equipped with winches to pull each other out of the deep, muddy ruts in the primitive road. After an arduous two-day journey over rough terrain, they arrived in Mistolar, the new home of the Nivaclé Latter-day Saints. They found a poverty-stricken people who had been stripped of every possession twice in the last two years. Tall weeds constituted the only walls of their homes, providing little protection against temperatures that plunged below freezing in the winter and soared above a hundred degrees most of the rest of the year. The nearest water supply was six miles away, but they had no buckets to transport the precious liquid. They were farmers, but were unable to plant because there was no rain, and they were barely able to keep themselves alive by hunting and fishing.

Despite these conditions, however, every member seemed in good spirits, and even the children were smiling and healthy.

The twenty-eight-year-old branch president, who spoke Spanish and the local dialect, met the visitors. "Are you well?" Elder Brewerton asked, realizing that the rice, beans, and salt his party had brought wouldn't last out the week.

"Yes, yes," he was assured.

"Are any among you sick?"

"We have thirty-nine priesthood bearers," the branch president said. "We bless our people and they don't get sick."

Elder Brewerton inquired about the faithfulness of the people and was told simply, "All are steadfast. We accepted the Lord when we were baptized. There is no way we could ever be inactive."

In a meeting that evening, the woman who gave the invocation seemed to echo the feelings of the congregation. Recounting their extensive losses and hardships, she asked the Lord to bless her people and concluded, "Father, we just want you to know that, no matter what happens, we will remain true and faithful because this is thy church." Greatly touched by all he saw, Elder Brewerton then dedicated their land, promising they would be blessed through their faithfulness.

Following his visit, the people planted their precious cache of seeds and found that the soil still held a little moisture, enough to tide them over until the rains came and they could sow and reap a full harvest. That winter the snowpack in the Andes mountains was twice as great as in previous years, indicating the annual floods would be worse than usual.

But the Nivaclé were not worried. "We won't be flooded this year," they said. "Our land has been dedicated by a servant of the Lord."

With the warmer season the raging waters overflowed their channels by as much as six miles, and twice they surged virtually to the doorsteps of the homes — and twice they receded. Safeguarded from the ravaging currents that had cost them so dearly in the past, these faithful Saints were able to nurture their gardens and provide themselves with a bountiful food supply.

"That was one of the most amazing experiences I've witnessed," said Elder Brewerton. "Those people are a great example to the rest of the Saints."

Through all of life's challenges, Elder Brewerton has remained decidedly optimistic, claiming, "I never get discouraged. I remember once about thirty years ago when I had a down moment that lasted about twenty seconds. I thought, 'So that's what depression is. I'm never going to have that again.' And I didn't."

That does not mean he has not faced difficulties or has avoided reality, but he has met problems squarely, relying on the Lord.

"The Lord won't leave us without help in the major decisions in life," he said. "My wife and I have had several experiences that involved major decisions and changes in our lives. But we have turned to the Lord, and there has always been a crystal-clear answer. I have tried to uplift myself and others, following the advice of a Frenchman who once said, 'When you write your history, take from the altars of the past the fire, not the ashes.' "

ANGEL ABREA

"Zion [is] all of North and South America, like the wide, spreading wings of a great eagle, the one being North and the other South America," President Spencer W. Kimball declared in general conference on April 4, 1975.

As a prophet with a great love for the peoples of Latin America and the insight to discern their vast potential, President Kimball was excited by the growth of the Church in that land. Perhaps it was that same enthusiasm—along with his zeal for building temples—that led him to take the unprecedented action of calling a president for the Buenos Aires Argentina Temple long before construction was under way and, in fact, almost four years before the temple would be in operation.

On March 20, 1981, a significant call came to the mission home of the Argentina Rosario Mission. The elder who answered the phone was told that someone in Salt Lake City wanted to speak to the mission president, Angel Abrea.

"Who in Salt Lake?" he asked curiously.

"President Spencer W. Kimball," was the startling reply that sent the excited young man hurrying to find his mission president.

When President Kimball requested that Sister Abrea also come on the line, President Abrea knew this was not a routine call. Though the phone connection was poor and the discussion left him puzzled, one thing was clear: the prophet had requested that he and his wife meet with him in Salt Lake City in just four days.

In the rush that followed — obtaining visas (a process that usually takes twenty days, but was miraculously accomplished in only one), making travel arrangements, packing suitcases — President Abrea had little time to contemplate the confusing phone call. But once in the air winging toward Salt Lake City with his wife, Maria, he had time to ponder the questions that swirled around in his mind. Had he heard correctly? Had President Kimball really called him to be a General Authority? A Seventy? Or had he asked him to be a temple president? A temple president — and his wife the temple matron — when there was no temple?

However, it was impossible not to understand one statement President Kimball had made. After asking how soon President Abrea was scheduled to be released from his mission — to which the answer was just over three months — the prophet had responded, "Now you will never finish your mission. *This* mission is for the rest of your life."

The next day in the office of the president of the Church, Angel Abrea and his wife discovered that he was indeed being called to be a General Authority — the first ever from Latin America. The native Argentine would become a member of the First Quorum of the Seventy, which had been organized five and a half years before. He was also being called as president of the temple to be constructed in Buenos Aires, but would serve in other capacities until it was completed, President Kimball explained.

Suddenly, everything in Elder Abrea's life was different. And yet, while all was new, nothing had really changed, because he had always been dedicated to the service of the Lord. "For this testimony, which is my surety, my rock, my sustenance, which I have received by the mediation of the Holy Ghost, I give infinite thanks, and I place all talents, time, efforts, and all that I possess to the work to which I have been called," he vowed in his first general conference address a few days later. (*Ensign*, May 1981, p. 28.)

This was not a new commitment, only a public affirmation of the standard by which he lived. Since his baptism into the Church at age ten, it had taken precedence in his life; everything that came after had been measured by that gauge. Being a General Authority would allow him to continue the full-time Church service begun with his call as mission president nearly three years earlier. It would not affect why or whom he served; it would only affect how and where.

Angel, the oldest of the two sons of Edealo and Zulema Estrada Abrea, was born September 13, 1933, in the sprawling Argentine metropolis of Buenos Aires. His heritage parallels that of many people in his native country, with a grandfather from Italy, another from Spain, and both his grandmothers born in Argentina. The Abreas were a close, loving family, whose principles of morality, integrity, and hard work were taught by example. Edealo and Zulema respected and supported each other as well as their sons, Angel and his brother, Oscar, who was seven years younger.

Edealo, a salesman and businessman with an interest in politics, once served as the mayor of a smaller Argentine city. Zulema, like her husband, was very proud of her children and encouraged them to succeed, convincing them of the importance of obtaining a good education. Though she wanted Angel to have some exposure to religion, she didn't want him to attend the Catholic Church, the religion of 90 percent of her countrymen. Instead she sent him to a Lutheran primary school and occasionally to Lutheran meetings on Sunday, where as much as half of the services would often be in German. But she was not really satisfied with that, and the family seemed to be "waiting for something to believe in," Elder Abrea recalled later.

Then one day Zulema invited in two sister missionaries from The Church of Jesus Christ of Latter-day Saints who had knocked on her door. She was immediately interested in their message and, at their suggestion, began reading the Book of Mormon with nine-year-old Angel. Though he didn't understand everything he read, he had a special feeling about the book. A year later, in 1943, Zulema and Angel were baptized. Oscar, then three years old, was baptized when he turned eight. Zulema and her sons attended all of their meetings, walking two miles to the rented house where the tiny local branch met.

From the beginning, Edealo Abrea fully supported his wife and sons and was a staunch defender of the Church, though he never became a member himself. Early one Sunday morning he taught Angel a valuable lesson. About a year after Angel's baptism, he woke up on a Sunday morning and decided he didn't feel like walking the distance to the meeting place. "I think maybe I'll stay home today," he informed his mother. Sitting on his son's bed, Edealo told his son, "Angel, if you are going to be a member of that church, you are going to have to be loyal to all of the covenants you made when you were baptized. You made a commitment, and you will have to honor it. Now get up, get dressed, and go to church."

To this day, Elder Abrea doesn't know why his father

never became a member. It was common in that time for an investigator to attend church services for many years before being baptized, and somehow Edealo seemed to get locked into that mode. He seemed comfortable with the idea that "it is good for you to be a member, but not for me," his son explained. When Spencer W. Kimball, then a member of the Council of the Twelve, called Elder Abrea as a stake president, he suggested that the new stake leader invite his father to the meeting where he would be sustained, and again when he was released and sustained to other positions. "My father came to many, many meetings and was always proud of his sons' accomplishments," explained Elder Abrea, adding wistfully, "I can't understand why we weren't bolder in challenging him to be baptized." Edealo Abrea died in 1976, and his son is convinced that he has since embraced the gospel. "I know he has, I feel it here," says Elder Abrea, laying a hand on his heart.

Though Zulema never succeeded in converting her husband, she was imbued with a missionary zeal that pushed her into sharing the gospel. It wasn't uncommon for her to begin a conversation with someone while seated on a bus or standing on a street corner, and the next Sunday the person would be in church. Over the years she has brought as many as forty-five converts into the Church, Elder Abrea estimates, including many who went on to serve in leadership positions, such as a regional representative, two stake presidents, four or five bishops, and a number of Relief Society presidents. Another of Zulema's loves was working with children, and she served more than thirty-five years in the Primary. When the Buenos Aires Temple opened, Sister Abrea, at age seventy-five, became a temple worker.

The 1940s was a difficult time to be a Latter-day Saint in Argentina; there were few books, manuals, or other materials, few facilities, and few members—only about four hundred in the entire country. It could have been especially tough for a teenager, but for Angel, belonging to a tiny minority was an adventure. He saw his Church membership as an advantage rather than a hindrance. Since the Church had come into his life, it *was* his life, and he couldn't imagine things any other way. Following his older brother's example, Oscar Abrea also became devoted to the Church and eventually served as a bishop, stake president, and institute of religion director.

Most of Angel's after-school hours were spent with LDS friends in Church or athletic activities; he played soccer with school teams and basketball with Church teams. Once when he was twelve, he was a member of a choir that was asked to sing at a mission conference. Although it took two hours for him to walk to the rehearsal location, an hour to sing, and two hours to walk back home, he was glad to be involved and excited about the conference, which would be attended by some three hundred members from all over the country.

The summer Angel was fifteen, he had his first hands-on experience with full-time missionary work and found it exhilarating. He spent his summer vacation as a stake missionary, whetting his appetite for missionary experiences to come. Looking back on his youth, he recognizes it as a time of both difficulty and joy—full of work and effort, yet important in shaping the pattern of his life.

After completing secondary school, Angel began studying accounting at Buenos Aires University and working in his father's business. He was soon using his newfound knowledge to pay his way through school by doing accounting for his father, then other clients.

Tutoring younger students was another way Angel met his educational expenses. One of those students was fourteen-year-old Maria Victoria Chiapparino, an intelligent, pretty girl. Ever alert for a chance to be a missionary, Zulema began inviting Maria to attend Church activities and was soon instrumental in teaching her the gospel. The following year Angel, then an eighteen-year-old priest, baptized her. He also began dating her, and a romance developed. On July 4, 1957, when he was twenty-three and she was eighteen, they were married. (Nine years later, on September 26, 1966, they and their three daughters were sealed in the Salt Lake Temple.)

Like Angel, Maria has been active in the Church. At twenty-one she was called as the mission Relief Society president, the first Argentine to hold that position. She also served five years as seminary teacher, rising each morning at four-thirty to prepare, then picking up her students and taking them to the church for class. Angel got up at five every morning to care for their three daughters while she was gone. "It was a challenge for the entire family," he admits. However, he proudly points to his wife's success as a seminary teacher: "She had twenty students during that time, and eighteen of them went on missions. Some were even sent to our mission. She is a great teacher. She loves the youth."

The early years of Angel and Maria's marriage were busy ones—for the Abrea family as well as for the Church in Argentina, which was growing rapidly. When they had been married three months, Angel was called as a branch president. Over the next several years he also served as a district president; a counselor to the mission president; president of the Buenos Aires Stake—the first stake president in his country; regional representative—the first Argentine to serve in that position; and president of the Buenos Aires West Stake. Also during that time the couple had three daughters, Patricia Viviana, Claudia Alejandra, and Cynthia Gabriela.

When Angel graduated from the university as a certified public accountant, he began working for Deloitte, Haskins and Sells, an international accounting firm. He felt that being a member of the Church was an asset to his professional career. Company officials were understanding about his heavy church involvement, and as his fellow employees came to know him, many went to him for advice or counsel on personal problems, and he became known as a sort of tongue-in-cheek "company bishop."

Elder Abrea's call to serve as a regional representative over regions in three different countries—Buenos Aires, Argentina; Lima, Peru; and Montevideo, Uruguay—necessitated a tremendous amount of time and travel. On many occasions he would leave town on Friday evening (often spending the night on a plane), attend meetings on Saturday and Sunday in a distant area, and travel home Sunday night, arriving on Monday morning, just in time to rush from the airport to his office. When his father died, he was scheduled to attend a conference in another country and had to catch a flight out of Buenos Aires just hours after the funeral. He was deeply shaken by his father's passing, and his daughter Cynthia, seeing his grief, asked why he didn't stay home. Elder Abrea reminded her that her grandfather had always urged him to live up to his commitments to the Lord. He would be honoring his father by going through with what was expected of him.

Elder Abrea's wife and children became accustomed to his busy schedule and learned to cope uncomplainingly with the problems that came up while he was away. One rare weekend when he was at home, one of his daughters asked her mother, "Why is Daddy at home?" Elder Abrea was deeply committed to his family, and when he was at home, he was totally at home, participating in such family outings as picnics in the park, going out to dinner and the theater, and attending Church activities. His young daughters occasionally enjoyed preparing special dinners for their parents. Angel and Maria would get dressed up, leave the house, drive around the block, and then "arrive" at home, where the girls would greet them, usher them into the house, and serve dinner. Angel also managed to participate in regular personal interviews with each of his daughters, frequent date nights with his wife, and family vacations to the seashore or a favorite mountain spot.

Following his father's example, Angel became involved in politics and served for a time as secretary of the treasury for San Miguel, a city near Buenos Aires with a population of about one million. But when he found that the time required for public service interfered with his Church commitments, he decided to leave politics and steer his career in other directions. It was a difficult decision, for he was an idealist who believed he had a lot to give his country, but he also knew that for at least that period in his life, it was not what he wanted.

Another opportunity to choose between government and Church service came several years later while he was a mission president. A representative of the president of Argentina contacted him and asked if he was available to accept a post as second in command over the nation's economy. The offer was especially attractive because President Abrea had left a good job when he accepted the mission call, and he didn't know what he would do when the three years were over. He sought advice from Elder Robert E. Wells, then serving as the Church's executive administrator for Argentina, who in turn took the problem to the First Presidency. The response was that President Abrea had permission to accept the job if he chose to do so. Again a difficult decision. After pondering and praying, he decided to decline the offer, preferring to finish his mission assignment and trust in the Lord for whatever would come next.

When Elder Abrea accepted the call as president of the Argentina Rosario Mission in 1978, he approached the assignment filled with a sense of purpose and urgency. No longer could missionaries be content with investigators who studied the gospel for months, sometimes years, before being baptized, as had often been the case. "*Now* is the time," he stressed. "We can't afford to wait that long."

"I gave up a lot of things in my life to be a mission president," he told the missionaries at his first mission conference. "I came here to be successful, but I will not be so until *you* succeed." Indeed, as the missionaries caught President Abrea's vision, they were successful and the number of baptisms in the mission increased from an average of 35 a month to 350 a month, and in some particularly fruitful months as many as 500. As the number of baptisms increased, soon up to 30 percent of the 185 missionaries were native Argentines; and where one stake had previously encompassed the whole mission, now the area was divided into six stakes. The mission's accomplishments were a reflection of what was taking place in Argentina as a whole, with an average of 1,800 new converts monthly in the country's five missions. For example, where there had once been one stake in the city of Buenos Aires, now there were ten.

As his years as mission president slipped by, Elder Abrea gave little thought as to what would come after. Though the officers of his accounting firm had respected his religious convictions, they couldn't understand why he would resign his job in order to take a nonpaying ecclesiastical assignment. Indeed, several others, including his daughters and some of the missionaries, asked what the family intended to do after his mission. His only answer was that he was unconcerned about it. He and Maria had resolved to leave their future in the hands of the Lord. Though they hoped to be able someday to serve in the temple, they had no idea how fully that desire was to be realized.

In early March 1981, Elder Abrea received a letter from the Church's Missionary Department, reminding him that he would soon be released and should be making preparations to return to private life. And just a week later, Elder and Sister Abrea received the phone call from President Kimball that would result in Elder Abrea's becoming the president of a temple to be constructed in his own country, as well as the first General Authority from Latin America. It was fitting that the call should come from President Kimball, for the bonds of love and respect were already strongly established between the two men. President Kimball had ordained Elder Abrea a high priest, set him apart as a stake president, called him to be a regional representative, and called him to be a mission president.

Until the new temple could be constructed, Elder Abrea would function in other capacities, he was told. After traveling to Salt Lake City for general conference, where he was sustained and set apart as a Seventy, he returned to Argentina to complete his mission and prepare to move to Utah. In July 1981, Elder and Sister Abrea moved to Salt Lake City. Their daughters, then ages nineteen, twenty, and twenty-two, remained at home in Buenos Aires, where they were enrolled at the university, until their visas came through, and then joined their parents in Utah. After living in Buenos Aires, with a population of 11 million, the Abreas enjoyed "small-town" life offered by predominantly Mormon Salt Lake City. Elder Abrea's first assignment as a Seventy was as executive administrator over Peru and Bolivia, responsibilities he fulfilled by commuting from Utah. In correlation with his status as a temple president-in-waiting, he also served as managing director of the Temple Department. In 1984, when the Church replaced all executive administrators with area presidencies, he was assigned to the Mexico Area presidency.

In August 1985, as the Buenos Aires Temple neared completion, the Abreas returned to Argentina. With the dedication scheduled for January 1986, they had several months to supervise the finishing details, call and train temple workers, and oversee the prededication open house. In this new calling they worked together. Once before, while he served as mission president, the couple had also had the opportunity to function side by side, an arrangement they found enjoyable and fruitful. During their almost thirty years of marriage, with Elder Abrea away from home a great deal because of involvement in church work and his profession, Maria Abrea had often found herself running the home and making all but the most critical decisions, as well as those that couldn't wait, on her own. "There is a need to learn to be alone many times, to share one's husband with many people," Sister Abrea said later, referring to those times. (*Ensign*, October 1984, p. 26.) Now their joy in working together was second only to their delight in the tasks before them.

If having a temple in their own country was a dream come true for the Abreas, it was equally so for thousands of faithful Argentine Latter-day Saints, for whom the nearest temple had been in Sao Paulo, Brazil. Yet, despite the thirty-eight-hour bus ride from Buenos Aires to Sao Paulo, Argentines had constituted the biggest group in temple attendance there.

"The announcement of a temple in Argentina was met with joy and thanksgiving," explains Elder Abrea. "Immediately local Church members began contributing all they could. When we opened the temple, seventy percent of those called to be temple workers had not been endowed themselves. We had to work with them in getting their own endowments and then teach them how to serve in the House of the Lord."

Elder Abrea saw much growth in the members as they sacrificed to attend regularly. He recalls with fondness one seventy-year-old woman who, despite a strike by local transportation workers, promised Sister Abrea she would be at her shift the following day. Though she had to ride fifteen miles on a bicycle each way, she was there, grateful and uncomplaining. Another sister, who had not had an oppor-tunity for an education, was willing to serve in any way needed, but, she begged, "Please don't make me an ordinance worker, because I don't know how to read." Perhaps she could stand at the door and greet people, she suggested. "Though this woman was unlearned, she had a special gift for spirituality," explains Elder Abrea. "I saw the hand of the Lord working with her and she became very effective, faithful, dedicated. Within six months she came to me crying with joy at being able to serve as an ordinance worker."

Tears run down Elder Abrea's cheeks and his voice softens to a hush as he speaks of the people and experiences that are so near his heart. "You have to know the people to understand this. Having a temple has given them a different perspective of the gospel and the plan of salvation. For many converts who had learned about temples almost since they learned about the Church, temple blessings had always been out of reach, something they would never be able to attain. And suddenly they had a temple in their midst."

After serving at the temple in Argentina for two years, Elder Abrea was assigned to Quito, Ecuador, as a member of the president of the South America North Area, an area that includes Ecuador, Bolivia, Peru, Colombia, Venezuela, French Guiana, Guyana, and Suriname. This time he and Maria traveled alone, for Patricia, Claudia, and Cynthia had each married by then. And, to their delight, the Abreas, who had only daughters, now have only grandsons, five of them. In the fall of 1989, Elder Abrea was again assigned to Salt Lake City, this time in the Utah South Area presidency and as assistant executive director of the Missionary Department.

When Elder Abrea was first called as a General Authority, the mantle of his calling weighed heavy on his shoulders, though he carried it willingly. He also recognized the responsibility inherent in being the first person from his continent to hold such a position. The members in Argentina, as well as the rest of Latin America, rejoiced in having one of their own among the Brethren. However, Elder Abrea has come to realize that he is not a representative of his people, but rather a worldwide ambassador for his Father in heaven. "My perspective has changed since 1981," he says. "I used to look at the Church from the South to the North; now I see it from the North to the South. It's an educational process, and I can better understand the concept of a worldwide Church.

"I used to ask myself, 'Why me?' There are so many uncertainties, so many expectations, and you always feel yourself unequal to the task. But you know you have been called by the Lord; that is the only assurance you need." His approach to his calling has been similar to his approach to his profession. "I am results oriented," he explains. "I want to improve, to make each day a little better than yesterday. I used to tell my missionaries to do their best every day, and then when their mission was over, when they got to the end of their road, they wouldn't have to say, 'I could have done better.' That's what we have always taught our daughters, and I think that is what makes a real family, everyone working together to do his best. It's the same for the Church."

As the years have passed, Elder Abrea has learned more of what to expect and what others expect of him. With many of his earlier uncertainties resolved, he has begun to feel more at home with his calling; he has matured and mellowed in the Lord's service, his natural reserve melting to a more patient, more outgoing persona. Though he still has feelings of inadequacy and incredulity that the Lord has chosen him, his resolve to serve the Lord is strong. Ever before him is the example of the prophet Nephi, on whom he has patterned his life since he and his mother first read the Book of Mormon

112

almost fifty years ago. "I have tried to be like Nephi," he explains, "to emulate his faith, which is simple, yet so profound. Nephi plainly says that the Lord has told us to obey. Therefore, we will not contend with him, we will obey."

And for the son of Zulema Abrea, nothing more need be said.

WALDO P. CALL

To a young boy growing up in Mexico, the prospect of testifying of the Savior to a multitude of people might seem a bit frightening, or even downright terrifying. But sixteen-year-old Waldo P. Call was undaunted by the promise given in his patriarchal blessing that thousands would hear his testimony. In fact, the blessing, given by his grandfather, was an inspiration, a noble target to aim for as he prepared for his mission.

During his two and a half years serving in the Mexican Mission in the late 1940s, Elder Call kept the goal uppermost in his mind, bearing his testimony at every opportunity. When he returned home his soul burned with a fervor that was intensified by those experiences. He knew his patriarchal blessing had been accomplished.

Twenty-four years later, when he was called as a stake

president, he often had opportunities to bear his testimony to the members of his stake, which numbered well over a thousand. "I felt certain the blessing had been more than fulfilled," he admits.

Then he became a regional representative, and many thousands more had the opportunity to be blessed by his testimony. And while serving as a mission president in Uruguay, he again thought the blessing had come to fruition in the fullest extent possible.

Now, in his calling as a member of the Second Quorum of the Seventy, the blessing is being realized to a far greater degree than the young Mexican farm boy, and probably even his patriarch grandfather, could ever have envisioned.

When he bore his testimony in general conference in April 1985, after having just been sustained as a member of the First Quorum of the Seventy, his simple yet powerful words, "I know that this is the work of the Lord. I know that he lives," were spoken to a worldwide audience of millions through radio, television, and satellite communications. It wasn't until then that he began to truly understand the significance and eternal scope of that blessing, a blessing that is continuing to bless his own life and the lives of countless others.

To the untutored observer, Elder Call's lean five-foot ten-inch frame, graying hair, and hazel eyes belie his roots; he neither looks nor sounds Mexican. He was born in Colonia Juarez, one of nine settlements founded by Church officials at the foot of the eastern slopes of the Rocky Mountains in northern Mexico in the latter half of the nineteenth century. (Only two of the original settlements still exist, Juarez and Dublan.) But although he was born of North American ancestry and grew up speaking English in a town full of two-story brick homes that looked remarkably similar to their Utah counterparts, Elder Call considers himself very much a Mex-

115

ican. "Mexico is my country, the land of my birth. I love it," he affirms.

That Elder Call would be called as a General Authority, whose duties take him around the globe, may seem again unlikely considering his beginnings. As one of thirteen children born to a struggling sharecropper, Waldo had never been more than a few miles outside of the colonies in the first eighteen years of his life. But to those who knew his parents, Charles Helaman and Hannah Skousen Call, maybe their son's call wasn't so surprising after all. Faced with raising their large family in the arid desert, the Calls dedicated their lives to the Lord, their family, and hard work—in that order. They instilled those same priorities in their children, lessons deeply ingrained in the younger Calls by the example of their parents.

Waldo Pratt Call, a great-great-grandson of Elder Parley P. Pratt, was born February 5, 1928, the third oldest of ten boys and three girls. "I always thought I was picked on because my friends could go play after school and on Saturdays, but I had to go home and work," he recalls. The farm, a few miles outside of Colonia Dublan, provided work aplenty for Waldo, whose chores included milking cows; working in the family garden and in the fields of alfalfa, wheat, corn, and beans; taking care of the pigs, chickens, and cows; helping make lard and soap; and washing dishes, ironing, and folding the seemingly endless piles of diapers. Most of the plowing and other farm work was done by hand or with horses, with the occasional use of a single communal tractor, and Waldo grew adept at planting corn with a stick.

The family was largely self-sufficient, eating what they grew and wearing clothes made by Hannah. And what the family couldn't provide, the tight-knit community did. With milk as a steady, though small, source of income, supplemented by seasonal harvests of other cash crops, the family would trade with the local merchants at the grocery, butcher, shoe, and saddle shops.

Although a water wheel in a nearby spring provided electricity for part of the town, the Call farm was about a mile past the end of the lines and so they had no electricity—or indoor plumbing—until Waldo returned from his mission. When the family outgrew the original three-room farmhouse, Charles added a porch along the back of the building, with adobe walls three feet high and screen from there to the ceiling. The older children were moved into the new addition, where, Elder Call recalls, "we just had to put on more of Mom's homemade quilts to keep warm." As the family continued to grow, a grain storage shed in the backyard was fixed up for a sleeping room for the older boys. "We never thought we were poor or neglected. We were in about the same situation as everybody else," Elder Call says. "And I never remember having to go hungry." Fare was simple, with meals consisting mainly of bread (Hannah baked about ten dozen loaves a month) and milk, fresh produce from the garden in season, canned fruit and vegetables in the winter, and the occasional treat of home-bottled pork or venison. A memorable meal came when Waldo's older sister, just home from a mission, insisted that they have hamburgers, a food she had sampled while away from home. "Dad drove into town and bought hamburger meat and that night we all had hamburgers," Elder Calls remembers. "I liked them."

As soon as Waldo became involved in church and school activities, those took precedence over his home chores, emphasizing the importance of an education and fulfilling his responsibility to the Lord. Although life in *las colonias* was rigorous and demanding, it was a happy setting for his childhood. That small home, overflowing with children, was also packed with love, spirituality, and learning. Evenings were often spent around the fireplace, talking and singing, and

117

every Saturday night reading the Book of Mormon while Charles repaired saddles and shoes with baling wire and buckskin tanned from deerhide and Hannah mended clothes and rocked babies. Music was an important part of the family's life, and Waldo learned to play the piano, trumpet, and guitar, and he even took violin lessons for a while, until the teacher moved away. "My parents said we could get up at five o'clock and either milk cows or practice the piano," he explains. "I opted for piano. I took lessons from a woman who came to our home, starting out with the only music we had, the hymns. One of my grandmothers wanted me to be a doctor, my mother felt I ought to be a pianist, but I always wanted to be a farmer."

In late summer, after the crops were in, the family would pack their things in a covered wagon and spend a week in the mountains, often inviting another family to go with them. Waldo reveled in the beauties of nature, and the annual outings are highlights of his childhood memories. During Christmas vacation from school, Charles would take his older sons to camp out and hunt game in the snow-covered mountains.

The lives of the residents of the two settlements were closely intertwined. Waldo was born in Colonia Juarez only because his mother's sister, who was a nurse and took care of Hannah during her confinement, lived there. But he was raised and attended grade school in Colonia Dublan. Long before he was old enough be a student, he would ride in the wagon to the school through the predawn hours with his father, who chopped kindling and built a fire in the school's wood-burning furnace, banking the coals so they would keep the students and teachers warm all day.

High school at the Juarez Stake Academy was a dusty, forty-five minutes away by bus. Though the school vehicle afforded little comfort and no warmth in the winter months, it was the pride and joy of the community, which had sent

Charles Call and two other men to Los Angeles to pick it up and drive it home.

In school Waldo developed fluency in both Spanish and English, an ability that would be advantageous in years to come. "He's not a gringo, he's a Mexicano," he often heard while serving as president of the Uruguay Montevideo Mission and as area president in South America. Doors were opened and paths made smooth because the people embraced him as one of their own.

In 1946 Waldo graduated from high school and moved to Provo, Utah, to attend BYU. He studied hard, held down a part-time job to pay for tuition, and spent a lot of time with Beverly Johnson, a fellow freshman whom he had met when her family moved to Colonia Juarez during their senior year in high school. That year at BYU Waldo received his mission call and was scheduled to leave in June. But when he and Beverly became engaged, he called the mission home in Salt Lake City and ask if his departure could be changed to September. At that time the Church allowed married men to be called on missions, and Waldo and Beverly wanted to get married before he left. Permission was granted, and the excited couple notified their parents of the upcoming nuptials and began to plan the wedding. But as they rode home from school together on the train, they decided that getting married just two weeks before the groom left on a mission was "a pretty dumb thing to do." The wedding would be postponed until Waldo returned from his mission. "I remember getting off the train and telling Dad that we'd decided to wait. 'I think that's a good idea,' he told me. But I was always glad that neither her parents nor mine had said anything, just let us work it out ourselves," Elder Call comments.

In the fall of 1947 Waldo left for the Mexican Mission. A year later Beverly was called to the same mission, and they saw each other many times during the next several months.

He was released in April 1950, and three months later she too was released. That August they were married in the Mesa Arizona Temple.

The newlyweds shared a love for music, and the afternoon after their wedding they went to a music store and bought a stack of music, mostly from Broadway musicals. "After that Beverly and I sang together a lot, mostly for our own enjoyment, but also at church meetings, weddings, and funerals."

The newlyweds lived for two years in Dublan, where Waldo taught school and their first child was born. In 1952 they returned to BYU. Waldo couldn't decide whether to study agronomy, music, or youth leadership/recreation, and he changed his major frequently. "But I happened to be caught in agronomy when I graduated, so that's what my degree is in," he says.

It was a difficult period, with too little time and money, and both were stretched almost to the breaking point. The Calls had three more children while they were in Provo, and Waldo divided his attention between classes, full-time employment, a Church calling or two, and his family. "I was always taught that you didn't work on Sunday, and if you were a student, studying was your work," he explains. "If you didn't get it all done on Saturday, you got up a little earlier Monday morning." He turned down jobs that would have required that he work on Sundays, including one that might have resulted in a lucrative and prestigious career, but would have required a lot of travel.

"We got married to be together, and never regretted the choices we made. All of the riches in the world weren't more important than that." Often the only time the young couple had together was when he would get home from work late at night. But they found they didn't need a lot of material comforts to make them happy. Sometimes in the evening they would take change from their money jar and walk the few blocks to the BYU dairy to buy ice cream cones, then return home arm in arm, laughing and talking, secure in their love and happiness.

After graduation the family moved back to Colonia Juarez, where Waldo began teaching school. He also farmed with his father-in-law in the evenings and on Saturdays, as well as many early mornings and during lunch hour. He planted orchards of peaches, pears, and apples, and in 1963 he left teaching to devote his time to a dream he held as a child: being a farmer. His Church callings during that time included choir director, scoutmaster, explorer leader, elders quorum president, bishop's counselor, and high councilor. From 1968 to 1979 he served as president of the Juarez Stake; from 1979 to 1982, as a regional representative; and from 1982 to 1985, as president of the Uruguay Montevideo Mission.

At the conclusion of their mission in Uruguay, the Calls had planned to return to Mexico, turn their farm over to their sons, and settle down in an area where they could serve in a temple. But their lives didn't go exactly as planned, for Elder Call was called in April 1985 to serve as a member of the First Quorum of the Seventy (four years later he became a member of the Second Quorum of the Seventy when that quorum was formed). His first assignment as a General Authority was to preside over the area encompassing Uruguay, Paraguay, Argentina, and Chile. "This will change our lifestyle completely, of course," he said in an interview for the *Ensign*."He always wanted to be of service more than anything else," Sister Call added. "It doesn't make a bit of difference what he's asked to do in the Church, he's ready."

"I feel very humble and weak [in this new calling]," he explained. "But I feel that we . . . can love the people. And we can teach them common sense in the gospel—basic gospel principles of faith, repentance, baptism, the gift of the Holy

Ghost, honesty, patience and love." (*Ensign*, May 1985, p. 92.)

Over the next eighteen months the Calls served again in South America, leading and teaching by exhortation, love, and example. When they returned to Salt Lake City for general conference in October 1986, little did Elder Call realize that this journey would be the last one he would take in this life with his beloved wife, Beverly.

For many years Sister Call had had heart problems. As a child an undiagnosed case of rheumatic fever weakened her heart, although the defects did not show up until she was pregnant with her seventh child in 1959. Her aortic valve had become encrusted with calcium deposits, preventing it from closing entirely.

Because of her rapidly deteriorating health, the baby was delivered at seven months by cesarean section. Though her new son weighed only about three pounds, he suffered no ill effects from either the early delivery or his mother's heart ailment. After a ten-day stay in the hospital in El Paso, Texas, both mother and baby were released. "We looked at this tiny thing in the incubator and said, 'How can we take him home?' " Elder Call relates. "But the doctor's attitude was, 'You've had six others, you know what to do.' So off we went, an eight-hour drive into Mexico over rough roads and far from a hospital, with this tiny baby. We thought many times since that we were either really dumb or really blessed to do what we did." (Jon Dana is now six feet tall and married, with four children of his own.)

Six months later Sister Call had heart surgery, a new and risky procedure in which the surgeon removed two ribs, spread her ribcage apart, and, through an incision directly into the heart, reamed out the calcium deposits around the valve. The surgery was successful and for the next twenty-seven years, with regular checkups, medication, and rest, she was able to lead a fairly normal life. A potentially fatal incident occurred when she caught pneumonia, but her recovery was satisfactory, and many around her were unaware of her condition.

However, the Calls had been warned that sometime in the future additional surgery might be necessary. On Monday, October 6, 1986, the day after conference ended, Sister Call underwent a physical examination and was told that the time had come: she would undergo surgery the next day.

On Tuesday, before she was taken to the operating room, Elder Call was alone with his wife. She expressed the desire that she not come out of the surgery as an invalid, asked him to convey her love to their children, and—just as they wheeled her out of the room—mouthed the words "I love you" to him. That expression of love was the last picture he would have of her in mortality.

The surgery, though it took longer than expected, was pronounced a success by the surgeon, and Elder Call had left the hospital and returned to his hotel room. Just minutes later he received an urgent summons to return to the hospital. When he arrived, a medical team was working to revive her, but their efforts were unsuccessful. Later he was told that the heart muscle was so deteriorated that it had simply torn apart.

Although Elder Call had lived for many years with the possibility that his wife might die as a result of her heart problems, when the time came he found himself unprepared to deal with the reality. He went through the next several days—informing friends and relatives, making arrangements, holding the funeral in Colonia Juarez, and returning to his duties in South America—in a state of shock.

"It was what the Lord wanted," he says now, his eyes glistening with tears. "We had anointed her, she had the combined prayers of the First Presidency, the Quorum of the Twelve, and the Seventies in their meetings that day, the

123

operation had been successful, and yet she died. The Lord permitted her to stay long enough to raise our seven children. We had spent a few days before general conference with our family in Mexico, and a new grandchild was born while we were there. Several people who were around her those last few days told me how she seemed so peaceful and serene, as if surrounded by a special spirit. If she did know what was coming to her, she never mentioned it to me. I believe death was sweet to her. It was her time to go."

Despite his acceptance of the Lord's will, when he returned home to his apartment in Buenos Aires he was terribly lonely. He received letters regularly from his children, but he found his biggest comfort came from prayer and gospel study. "The Book of Mormon helped me more during that time than anything else," he recalls.

As he resumed his busy schedule, immersing himself in the endless array of details and obligations, he found himself longing for a helpmeet with whom he could share love and companionship and who would also help share some of the responsibilities required of a General Authority and his wife. Time and again he found his thoughts returning to LaRayne Whetten, a shy schoolteacher in Colonia Juarez. LaRayne and her family were long-time acquaintances of the Calls; shortly after Waldo and Beverly were married, Beverly had been LaRayne's Laurel teacher in MIA; and as her stake president, Elder Call had counseled LaRayne to leave Colonia Juarez and find a husband. "You'll never find one in this small place," he had told her. ("I'm glad now she never took that advice," Elder Call now says.) During the years the Calls served in South America, LaRayne always sent birthday and Christmas cards to them and to other missionaries. And, in fact, she taught several of the Calls' grandchildren in grade school. But with very little opportunity to communicate with her, let alone begin any kind of courtship, Elder Call prayed,

"If she's the one, will you soften her heart so she will accept me?"

"And the Lord did soften her heart," he explains, "but it wasn't easy."

"When I started getting these thoughts that I was going to be his wife, I thought I was imagining things," LaRayne says, picking up the story. "If you had the feeling that a General Authority was going to ask you to marry him, would you believe it? I couldn't imagine why I was feeling that way, that out of anyone in the Church, he would ask me. Besides, I didn't want all of the responsibility I knew I would have if I married him."

LaRayne tried to thrust the idea out of her mind, refusing to even consider the possibility. Months later, on a beautiful early spring day, she was walking on a hillside on the family ranch, feeling overwhelmed by the beauties of nature and gratitude for all that the Lord had given her. Kneeling in prayer, she placed herself in the Lord's hands, promising, "I'll do whatever it is you want me to do . . . "

"Even if it means marrying *him*," Elder Call interjects, finishing her sentence.

"I didn't say that," she protests, and both of them laugh.

Not long after that, Elder Call, again in Salt Lake City for general conference, phoned LaRayne and, with few preliminaries, proposed.

"Yes, I've been prepared for this," she answered.

"Next week?" was his next question. It didn't happen quite that soon. LaRayne wrapped up the year-end details at school, and in June 1987 she became the wife of Waldo P. Call. Within a week the newlyweds were in Buenos Aires, attending meetings in which the new bride was to participate.

Although she has found the transition to being Elder Call's wife remarkably easy ("It has been a miracle," she says. "We have had almost no adjustments to make"), becoming the wife of a General Authority has been even more overwhelming than she anticipated. Wives of the area presidencies are set apart as area representatives of the general boards of the Relief Society, Primary, and Young Women. Most women married to General Authorities don't suddenly acquire these callings, but have the chance to become accustomed them gradually. Sister Call literally plunged in headfirst — one day a reserved teacher at a small grade school in Mexico, and the next day the wife of a leader in a worldwide church and charged with instructing the local leaders of the women's auxiliaries in South America.

An incident shortly after Sister Call arrived in Buenos Aires illustrates the suddenness with which she assumed her new roles. The first weekend in August was a stake conference, over which Elder Call was presiding. Sister Call's assignment was to conduct two hours of leadership meetings in which she would instruct the stake auxiliary leaders. She would have generally had help, but Elder Call's counselors in the area presidency had received new assignments elsewhere, and the new counselors had not yet arrived. She was given a manual with a few basic instructions, but very little else. She was petrified.

"LaRayne had never been one to meet people," Elder Call explains. "She'd rather stay out on the ranch on her horse than attend a social, and if you asked her to speak in Church, she would need weeks to prepare and get her courage up."

"I had no idea what to do," says Sister Call. "I had never even been to one of those meetings, let alone taught one." She started by prayerfully studying the manual, but as the day of the conference came closer, she still didn't know what to do. So she began to fast, and she prayed and studied even harder. Finally, the day before the conference, she sat down and wrote out the things she felt she should teach. After the meetings, she felt good about the way everything had gone.

126

The following October she attended her first general conference in Salt Lake City with her husband. As she went to a Relief Society workshop held in conjunction with the conference, she listened as Sister Barbara Winder, general Relief Society president, told the leaders what they were supposed to teach—exactly what Sister Call had presented two months before. She heard a voice in her mind saying clearly, "See, I knew what I wanted you to do, and this is what you've been doing." The same affirmation came to her in the Primary and Young Women workshops. "I didn't know what I was supposed to do, but the Lord knew. Because I was able to listen to him, I taught the things he wanted," says Sister Call, her voice trembling with a mixture of gratitude and incredulity. "That's a really comforting feeling—to know the Lord is helping you. But it's pretty challenging to live in such a way as to continue to have his help."

Another new experience for LaRayne has been hosting visiting members of the First Presidency and the Council of the Twelve in her home. "It scared me just to have them there and to cook for them, when I have never done anything like that before," she admits. "I could not have met all of these new challenges without the Lord's help. And without the support of my husband, I couldn't have done it either. Of course, without him, I wouldn't have had to," she adds, laughing.

"President Marion G. Romney said years ago that we never have to make a mistake if we learn to live our lives by the Spirit," says Elder Call. "The difficulty is not in receiving revelation, but in recognizing when we have received revelation and then living by it. When we do the things that the Spirit tells us to do, then we have great success."

Elder and Sister Call haven't quite decided what they'll do at the end of his service as a member of the Second Quorum of the Seventy. They may return to Colonia Juarez, for many of their children and grandchildren are there, and they will always feel drawn to the homes, fields, orchards, and hills of their earlier lives. They would also like to live near a temple where they could participate in regular, frequent temple work. But whatever they are doing, one can be sure that Elder Call will also be continuing a practice that has become a life-long tradition for him: giving voice to his testimony of the gospel of Jesus Christ.

HELIO DA ROCHA CAMARGO

One morning in 1956, a young Methodist minister knocked on the door of the LDS mission home in Sao Paulo, Brazil. Introducing himself to the mission president, the young man explained that students at the College of Theology where he was enrolled were studying the doctrines of small religious groups outside the mainstream of Christianity. He and his colleagues were looking for someone who could answer questions on Mormon theology. Could the mission president come the following week to address the school?

President Asael T. Sorensen explained that he could not come at that time, but he would send two missionaries to explain their religion.

"Oh no, you'd better come yourself," the pastor cautioned. He explained that the gathering would consist of about fifty students and professors, all very learned, many with doctorate degrees in theology. Two inexperienced missionaries would not be equal to the job.

"Don't be alarmed," President Sorensen assured him. "I'll send two good boys."

The mission president was true to his word. When the two missionaries showed up at the seminary, however, what most impressed the young minister, who had been asked to conduct the meeting and introduce the visitors, was their size — they were both well over six feet tall. One of the elders, David Richardson, wrote later, "When we entered the auditorium our hearts almost failed us, for we saw about fifty ministers waiting eagerly for us. But calling silently upon the Lord once again for inspiration and support, we commenced the discussions." (*Church News*, August 26, 1978, p. 16.)

Despite the minister's earlier fears, the two were indeed equal to the task. They preached for over an hour, explaining the basics of Mormonism by combining the first three missionary discussions. They then concluded their sermon with a challenge for all present to be baptized.

After the missionaries left, several of the theologians said, "Those Mormons are crazy. They believe in funny things." They were amused that the two young men would think that these ministers, who were much older and more learned, would consider joining their church.

"We weren't impressed much with the doctrines," explained the minister who had invited them. "We really couldn't understand the consequences of what they were saying. But we were impressed with their courage and dedication. The conviction they had was astonishing. We had no doubt that they believed that what they had told us was true." The missionaries left behind not only a good impression, but also copies of the Book of Mormon and *A Marvelous Work and a Wonder*.

Although no one took the missionaries' baptism challenge

seriously, the seeds had been sown, seeds that would flourish in years to come and yield a rich harvest of conversions and baptisms far beyond the confines of that room. One of those with a tiny seed planted deep in his heart — although he didn't know it at the time — was the young minister himself, Helio da Rocha Camargo.

Helio had entered the seminary three years earlier, searching not only for an occupation but also for an answer to many questions about religion. He was certain that with the opportunity for in-depth study, his doubts would be resolved. After the missionaries' visit, he forgot the religion they had described, his thoughts focused on matters at hand. But soon after, another issue came up that was not so easily dismissed, that of infant baptism. "I had studied a great deal about this topic and just couldn't accept the doctrine," he explained. "Why did an infant need to be baptized? What sins had a baby committed?"

He went to his supervisor and told him that if a family brought their baby to be baptized, he could not, in good faith, perform the ceremony. His supervisor counseled that when that situation occurred, he should take the family to another minister to perform the ordinance. But this was not an answer Helio could accept. He believed that there was no scriptural basis for the practice of infant baptism, and that he would have to explain to the family there was no need for their child to be baptized. The supervisor responded that if this was his attitude, he couldn't possibly be a Methodist minister. This struck a responsive chord inside Helio, who had begun to suspect that he was not cut out for this occupation.

When his beliefs became known, Helio was summoned before a seminary council of teachers and officers. There he was told that, feeling as he did, he should not be a minister, and therefore he should not be a student there. But they were willing to give him a chance to recant. He was told to take a few months to investigate the issue at length and then to come back to report his findings.

Helio invited many of his teachers and colleagues to assist him in his study, but most declined. "What good would it do?" they asked. "You will never change your mind."

"But I want to change my mind," he responded. "I want to find good reason to change it."

He approached another teacher, who was also a good friend. "If this doctrine is true, I will be a minister," he told his friend. "But if it is not, I will have to find another direction to my life." So the two men began a concerted study, going back to scriptural sources and original texts in Greek whenever possible. After many weeks of searching, study, and discussion, the two met again. "You are right," the teacher said. "There is no scriptural basis for the doctrine of infant baptism."

"What could I do?" Elder Camargo asks now. "I just couldn't feel right about taking the infants to another minister to be baptized, as I was advised to do. To me that was not a satisfactory solution. So I returned to the council and told them how I felt, and they kindly invited me to leave the school."

By this time more than half of the students had become involved with the problem, and many had similar unresolved questions. Most decided that, although they couldn't understand the reasons, they would accept the doctrine of infant baptism on its face value. Three students, including Helio Camargo, could not and left the ministry. Each would eventually join The Church of Jesus Christ of Latter-day Saints and would become a powerful leader in the Church in Brazil.

Once he left the ministry, Helio was more determined than ever to find some answers. He began studying the doctrines of churches that did not baptize infants. As part of this study he started reading the book that the missionaries had given him months before, *A Marvelous Work and a Wonder*, by LeGrand Richards. He soon put away other materials, as he found this book contained the answers to all of his questions and even some of which he hadn't yet been aware.

He also began attending meetings of a different denomination every Sunday. One Sabbath morning he went to the center of Sao Paulo to attend a Lutheran service. The cathedral was large and impressive and filled to capacity with worshippers and beautiful music, but the words and lyrics were in German, a language he couldn't understand, so he quietly walked out after a few minutes.

As he left the services he realized he was in the vicinity of the place where he'd been told the Mormons held their meetings. He found the gathering, a handful of people meeting in a humble rented place — a far cry from the grand setting he had just left. But it was in these modest surroundings that he finally found what he had been seeking. Helio Camargo would no longer attend meetings in a wide variety of faiths; he would no longer spend countless hours searching the literature of many churches; he would no longer struggle to make sense of the mass of confusion and yearning that consumed him. Although it would still be months before his fledgling testimony would become the staunch bulwark that would fortify countless others, his restless soul had found a secure berth amidst the turbulence.

Elder Camargo's conversion was the culmination of a journey of religious dedication that had begun many generations before, with his ancestors. The first Camargo to emigrate from the Old World left Spain on a ship bound for Peru, but when the ship docked at a Brazilian port, he fell in love with the vast country and decided to stay. In his adopted land he found himself in the minority as a Spaniard in a country populated largely by Portuguese.

Elder Camargo's maternal grandparents, devout Presbyterians, reared their thirteen children on a farm in Resende, Brazil. Determined that their children would be well-educated, they advertised in a Methodist newspaper for a teacher who would live with them and instruct their children. Jose Medeiros de Camargo answered the ad and began teaching the Rochas' children. It wasn't long before he fell in love with one of the girls, Else Ferreira da Rocha.

When Jose and Else were married, her father, eager to keep his daughter close by, offered them a parcel of his farmland. They stayed there for several years and their four children were born there. But Jose wanted to study engineering, so eventually he took his family to Juiz de Fora, where he taught at a Methodist college while studying at a neighboring university.

Helio, who was born on February 1, 1926, was a year old and the youngest of the children when his family moved to the city. His early childhood was a happy time of family togetherness and growth. "Although my father was a teacher, and well-educated, I believe my mother taught me many important things, too," he says. Both parents felt the need to teach their children about a wide diversity of topics, and discussion around the dinner table was always animated and interesting. Music played an important part in their home, and they planned frequent outings to parks, zoos, and museums. Else converted to Methodism soon after her marriage, and the family attended church regularly. Jose often taught in Sunday school and conducted choruses.

Though Helio was raised in a city, he always had the country in his blood. As he grew up, he relished visits to his grandparents' home in Resende, where he rode horses, swam in the river, and learned the value of hard work and industry. In 1935 the family moved to Sao Paulo, where Helio's father taught at a local college. Just three years later Jose Camargo died of a minor infection that could have been easily cured today. Twelve-year-old Helio felt the loss keenly, for his father, an intelligent, loving man, greatly influenced his life. "I believe that he would have readily accepted the gospel, had he lived," he says. "In fact, he has been baptized and had all of his temple work done by proxy. I feel sure that he has accepted it."

Life changed drastically for the Camargos after Jose's death. Else's father told his daughter, "If you come home, I will take care of you and your children." Although the offer was tempting, she elected to stay in Sao Paulo and worked hard to remain independent. The family moved from their large, comfortable home to a small one on the outskirts of the city. Helio's oldest brother was studying engineering, and Else felt strongly that he should finish college, so she took a job, as did her sixteen-year-old daughter.

When Helio was seventeen, he entered the Academia Militar de Agulhas Negras (Brazil's equivalent of the U.S. Military Academy at West Point), which was in Resende. To be near him, Else at last accepted her father's offer and moved back to the old family home in 1943.

While Helio was on a school break, his sister offered to line up dates for him with some of her friends. "She introduced me to many girls, but there was only one who interested me," he claims. Nair Belmira de Gouvea, a pretty, dark-haired sixteen-year-old, was immediately attracted to the handsome cadet. They enjoyed going to dances and outings, but they also enjoyed studying the scriptures together, an activity that set a healthy precedent for the future they were planning. Because the Brazilian army would not allow non-commissioned academy students to marry, they were content to postpone any marriage plans.

On the day he was commissioned, Helio was engaged in training exercises on the Argentine border, two thousand miles from Resende. A fellow officer stumbled, and the pistol he was carrying discharged, discharging a bullet that struck Lieutenant Camargo in the abdomen and lodged in his spine. Gravely injured, for almost a month he hovered between life and death. His mother and Nair flew to his side and, when he was well enough to travel, accompanied him back to Resende.

Elder Camargo is convinced his life was saved because the Lord wanted him in His church. "I trusted in God, although I didn't know him very well," he says. The accident cut short his military career and set him on a path that would eventually lead him to the gospel.

As soon as Helio was well enough, he and Nair were married, and together they faced two long, difficult years of therapy and recuperation. Helio also took advantage of that period to teach himself English and Spanish. The newlyweds' future seemed tenuous at best, for Helio was removed from active service and made an instructor at the academy, where he attained the rank of captain. Though in time the injury healed almost completely, and today he has only an occasional limp in his left leg and diminished movements in the left foot, he knew his military career was over.

Another setback during that time of recovery was the heartbreaking stillbirth of their first child. A second child, Fernando, was born less than a year later, about the same time Helio was discharged from the army and returned to civilian life. Unsure what the future held, the Camargos moved to Sao Paulo, where he worked for a bank and then a steel company while he studied business administration. This was a busy time for the young family, and during the next eight years they had five more children—four sons and a daughter.

Though Helio found great joy in his growing family, his work was unfulfilling, and a deep hunger filled his soul. He believed the answers lay within his Methodist religion and

136

that he could find them by immersing himself in it. Thus, in 1953 he made another career change and decided to prepare to become a minister by enrolling at the seminary. He was soon an ordained minister with his own congregation, though he continued his program of study at the Methodist seminary, intent on becoming a doctor of theology. It was this circuitous path that brought him to the LDS mission home three years later, searching for some information about Mormonism.

As he studied the gospel, Helio was especially impressed with one elder who taught the Camargo family. The elder told them of his family's struggle to keep him on a mission, but his threadbare suit and worn-out shoes told them even more.

"This is not a rich American," Helio told Nair. "This is a poor American. Yet he spends two years away from his home to teach us the gospel." Again the humble dedication of missionaries was influential in his conversion.

One of the students who was expelled from the seminary at the same time as Helio was Walter Guedes de Queiroz. He lived for a short time with the Camargos and also began investigating the Church. He soon became a member (he has since served as a bishop, stake president, and mission president), and two months later, on June 1, 1957, Helio was baptized. That August Nair too joined the Church. She was pregnant for the seventh time, and shortly after her baptism their last child, Milton, was born. As each of the children turned eight, they were also baptized.

Adjusting to the LDS lifestyle was not difficult for the Camargos, for they had never smoked or drank, had already been paying tithing and attending meetings for several months, and lived a family-centered life of morality and hard work.

About a year after his baptism, Elder Camargo was asked to speak at a youth conference, where he encountered the third student who had been expelled from the seminary, Saul

Messias da Oliveira. Saul's wife was involved with a road-show production at the conference, and both were investigating the Church. Saul had many gospel questions for his old classmate and also wanted to return his copy of *A Marvelous Work and a Wonder*, which he had borrowed. Since leaving the seminary Saul had become the minister for a Presbyterian splinter group. Then, according to Elder Camargo, "he started reading my book and began to preach out of it to his congregation, and the people were accepting it. When he finally told them he could no longer be their minister because he was going to be baptized into the Mormon church, about sixty to seventy percent of his congregation followed and were also baptized."

About that same time the Camargos began noticing that their one-year-old son, Milton, was unable to move normally and couldn't put any weight on his legs. A doctor told them their baby might have polio. Elder Spencer W. Kimball, then a member of the Council of the Twelve, was visiting in Brazil, and Elder Camargo asked if he would administer to his child. He did so, assisted by the mission president, William Grant Bangerter (who later was called to the First Quorum of the Seventy). When Elder Camargo came home from work the next day, he found Milton standing happily in his crib, with no sign of pain. "President Kimball was always very special to our family," says Elder Camargo, his eyes shining.

At the time the Camargos joined the Church, Brazil had fewer than a thousand members, and in Sao Paulo there were only two small branches. By 1990 Church membership in that country was quickly approaching 350,000. Members of the Camargo family have been instrumental in that growth. Through the years Sister Camargo served in many positions, including teacher and president in the auxiliaries, and Elder Camargo served as a teacher, bishop, counselor to two mission presidents, stake president, mission president, district president, and regional representative. Their five surviving children (one son was killed at the age of twenty-one in an automobile accident) were all married or sealed in the temple and have held many leadership positions.

A choice experience came when the family traveled to Switzerland to meet their son Paulo Sergio, who had just completed a mission in Italy, and were sealed in the Swiss Temple. It was their first opportunity to visit a temple, many years before construction of the Sao Paulo Temple would be announced.

After leaving the Methodist seminary, Elder Camargo worked in management at several large companies and finally launched his own poultry equipment manufacturing business. He then became a poultry farmer, with more than thirty thousand hens, on some picturesque acreage in the mountainous countryside outside Resende.

In early 1985 Elder Camargo was released from his calling as a regional representative. One day while he was working on his farm, he received word that someone from Church headquarters was trying to reach him. He immediately came in from the fields and returned the call. It was President Gordon B. Hinckley. After inquiring about Elder Camargo's family, his business, and his Church service, President Hinckley asked what would happen to Elder Camargo's business if he were to leave it for a few years.

"Nothing very much," was the response. "My son is working with me, and he can handle it. Why?"

"Come to Salt Lake for general conference and I'll tell you," President Hinckley replied.

Elder Camargo called his wife to tell her they would be going to Rio de Janeiro the following day to get their passports in order, then flying to Salt Lake City. As they flew toward the United States, they talked nervously between themselves. What would it be — another mission call? a second calling to

serve as regional representative? The idea of being called to
serve as a General Authority wasn't given much thought—
surely *he* would not receive such a calling.

But when President Hinckley told them that indeed, the
Lord did wish to call him as a General Authority, Elder Camargo was immediately consumed with feelings of inadequacy. However, he had never turned down a calling from
the Lord; acceptance had always been immediate, followed
by diligent effort to do his best. He was not about to change
any old habits at this crucial time.

"When the Lord calls there is no option," he told President
Hinckley. "The only thing I can say is yes, although I am
unprepared."

Standing in the Salt Lake Tabernacle on April 6, 1985,
shortly after he was sustained as a member of the First Quorum of the Seventy, Elder Camargo addressed the gathering
on Temple Square and millions of members around the world.
"I don't know how my legs support my body now; this is an
experience I never wanted to have," he admitted. "When
President Hinckley called me and asked me to accept this
calling, there came to my mind the remembrance of a time
in the history of the people of God, Israel, when they had to
face their enemies. They assembled a huge army of strong
soldiers and they presented themselves in front of the Lord
to go to battle, and the Lord didn't accept this army. He
reduced it, and he reduced it again and again until only three
hundred people were left. And with this ridiculous army he
defeated the enemy and destroyed the enemies of his people.

"This is the way I feel about my calling in this position.
The Lord chose to put me in this position, using my weakness
and my inability so that he could prove that he is God, he is
the Lord, he is in charge. Even using my poor and broken
English, he can do his work." (*Ensign*, May 1985, p. 85.)

Humility is one of the characteristics Latter-day Saints in

Brazil, and now those around the world, have come to love and appreciate in Helio Camargo. Other familiar characteristics are his warm, self-deprecating humor as well as his love and appreciation for his companion, Nair. Shortly after he was sustained, he displayed both facets in a single comment made to the *Church News:* "I never thought about myself as a General Authority of the Church, but I always knew my wife had what it takes to be the wife of a General Authority." (*Church News,* June 16, 1985, p. 4.)

One of the aspects of this calling that Elder Camargo enjoys most is the association with other General Authorities. An experience he had before joining the Church makes the association even sweeter, bringing the opportunity into clearer focus.

While he was investigating the Church, an acquaintance who had met the Mormon missionaries before he did told him, "I think that the missionaries are sincere, but their leaders are not. The leaders know that the church is not true and just try to convince the others, keeping them from finding out the truth about the Mormon church."

When Camargo told his friend he was considering joining the Church, his friend replied, "Go ahead. After a few years you will discover that this is a church just like any other, and that what I said about their leaders is true."

Some time later the two friends happened to meet on the street and lunched together. "How long have you been a member of the Mormon church?" his friend asked.

"Three years."

"Okay, now you can tell me the truth about the Mormons."

Elder Camargo told his friend that the Church was true and that he should be baptized.

"Oh, you have become a fanatic," the friend said.

Elder Camargo told his friend that "the leaders are every

141

bit as sincere as the the missionaries, some much more so. They are men of God." This testimony has grown stronger as he has had opportunities to associate with modern-day prophets of the Church.

Since his call, Elder Camargo has served as a counselor in the presidency of the South America North Area, which encompasses Brazil, Ecuador, Peru, Bolivia, Colombia, and Venezuela. In October 1989 he became the area president. The explosive growth of the Church in this area has resulted in many challenges. One of the main concerns is to find members with enough experience and knowledge about the workings of the Church to lead their fellow members. But what the people lack in experience is more than compensated for by their faith and commitment to the gospel. "There are members living in Lima, Peru, who must travel ten to twelve days by train, bus, and boat to visit the temple in Sao Paulo," explains Elder Camargo. "Many have barely enough money to return home, and in some cases, they have sold everything they have to make the trip."

Among the poor peoples of South America, the seeds of the gospel find rich soil, prepared for the planting. "The scriptures say the gospel is to be preached to the poor," explains Elder Camargo. "They accept it more easily, and it isn't difficult to understand why. It is easier to enter the house of a poor person than to enter a condominium with security guards at the door. When some of the more affluent people hear of the gospel, all they can see is what they will lose by joining the Church—friends, position, status, respect. But the poor aren't blinded by what they'll lose, so this allows them to see all they have to gain by accepting the gospel."

Elder Camargo once wrote of his life, "I would compare my spiritual life with the peaceful spectacle of sunrise, where at first there is no marked distinction between darkness and light. But the darkness constantly recedes while gradually the light grows brighter, making shapes more distinct, colors more vivid, until there shines the full brilliance of the sun, the perfect day." (Hartman and Connie Rector, *No More Strangers*, 2 [Bookcraft, 1973]: 104.)

Now, reflecting on his calling as a Seventy, Elder Camargo says, "The Lord gives challenges to different people at different times. To some it is the challenge to help others, to do things only they would be able to do. To others it is the challenge to rise to the level of the position they have been called to, to prepare and refine themselves. This is the challenge he has given me. There are many leaders in Brazil who could serve in this calling as well as I can, or better. But the Lord has called me—for reasons no one but he can say—and so here I am."

DOUGLAS J. MARTIN

"If ye have desires to serve God, ye are called to the work."
(D&C 4:3.)

A desire to serve was pulsating in every fiber of Douglas Martin as he sat in the Salt Lake Tabernacle on Temple Square, the prophet's voice penetrating his very soul. President Spencer W. Kimball was urging older couples to devote a year or two of their lives to the Savior in the mission field, and Elder Martin was ready to heed the Lord's call.

When he returned home to New Zealand from general conference, he repeated the message to his wife, Wati. Immediately they began preparing for full-time missionary service. They decided that Elder Martin, a regional representative and patriarch of the Hamilton New Zealand Stake, would retire in four years, when he turned sixty.

As the designated time approached, the details were falling neatly into place, and Douglas and Wati Martin eagerly anticipated the coming changes. But the mission the Lord had planned for them was a little different from the one they were preparing for.

On a Sunday morning in late March 1987, Elder Martin received a call from President Gordon B. Hinckley. The First Presidency had tried for several days to contact him, but the Martins had just returned the night before from a short holiday surfing at the beach, one of Elder Martin's passions. President Hinckley told Elder Martin that he was being called to the First Quorum of the Seventy. When he set him apart a few weeks later, he commented, "That's the last time you'll be on the beach for a long time."

"It didn't really sink in at first," recalls Elder Martin. "But when he said I would be a General Authority, suddenly the impact hit me. I hung up the phone and told my wife. We sat in total silence and cried together for several minutes." They were humbled and moved by the calling, and also by the fitting way the Lord had readied their lives to accept the change.

"How grateful we are that we heeded the whisperings of the Spirit when listening to President Kimball several years ago!" said Elder Martin in general conference shortly after being sustained as a member of the First Quorum of the Seventy. (*Ensign*, November 1987, p. 23.)

Heeding the whisperings of the Spirit has shaped Elder Martin's life, seasoning the untried, lonely boy yearning for security and belonging and turning him into a stalwart servant of the Lord. The aching, empty spaces that characterized his early life have been filled by the peaceful reassurance of gospel and eternal family relationships.

At age two, Douglas came to live with George and Jessie Martin, a childless couple who had immigrated to Hastings, New Zealand, from the Scottish highlands several years before. The little boy, who had been given up for adoption by his young unwed mother, was received into the Martins' God-fearing Presbyterian home, where solid values of honesty, hard work, and firm discipline prevailed. Douglas was taught to pray as soon as he began to talk, and he grew up with an appreciation for the value of a shilling and an honest day's work.

But the little family was plagued with problems. Jessie's health was poor, and she was often hospitalized or confined to her bed for weeks at a time. George was unable to find work as a mechanic, his chosen field, and worked for some years on the night shift in a large slaughterhouse and meat-packing company. And so, although Douglas knew his parents loved him and tried to make the most of their time together, he was often left to fend for himself, spending afternoons and evenings alone. "Dad would leave me a little money to go and buy meat pies for supper," Elder Martin remembers. "On one occasion when I was about six, I saw a sign that said 'Eskimo Pies.' When I bought one, I was astonished to find there was ice cream inside."

Cheerful and optimistic by nature, Douglas grew independent and—never having known anything else—was not unhappy with his often solitary existence. But within his boyish heart stirred a yearning for stability and belonging, a hunger that would remain with him for years to come.

With Jessie's ill health, compounded by the bleak depression years, finances were always a concern. While Douglas was never sent out by his parents to get a job, he was industrious and enterprising and began working after school and on weekends while still young. As a schoolboy he picked peas in the fields for a nearby cannery, then went on to hoeing and weeding mangles (sugar beets), spraying fruit trees, picking fruit, cleaning wooden floors with sawdust and kerosene in a large clothing store, and having a paper route.

146

Despite the long hours spent working, he found time to be outdoors, developing interests that would last a lifetime. He loved to swim and body surf, and when he wasn't at the beach he could be found in the mountains, enjoying hunting with a rifle, fishing, camping, or just hiking. But his overriding passion was for rugby—"the only *real* game," he claims. When he was twelve, he tried out for a rugby team, comprised of the best players in Hastings, to compete against teams from other towns for a regional trophy. The top players were chosen from each school; then from these dozens of finalists, the team was selected. Although he was one of the youngest (the age limit was fourteen) and the lightest (his weight of one hundred pounds was well under the limit of one hundred sixteen pounds), he survived the final cuts and practiced with the team for weeks.

Finally, the night before the first game, his coach came to him and said that they had decided to cut the team by one more player, and Douglas wouldn't be needed. Brokenhearted, Douglas rode home on his bike, tears streaming down his face. But the experience didn't quell his enthusiasm for sports, which he continued to play for years.

"I learned a valuable lesson that has stayed with me," he says. "You don't get everything you want in life. Because I learned that when I was twelve, I've never felt disappointed from that day till now if I've been passed over for something. It's not a lesson that I regret."

For a while his father drove a sheep truck, and Douglas would go out on the road with him, cherishing the time they spent together. George Martin was a quiet, kindly, but undemonstrative man who, despite his love for his son, had little in common with him. As Douglas became increasingly involved in athletics and outdoor activities—interests his father did not share—they each tended to go their own way. And although he was close to his mother, her poor health kept her out of her son's busy life. Thus Douglas was continually disappointed that neither of his parents ever went to his swimming meets or rugby games. This gap was filled to some extent by holidays spent with an uncle and aunt who shared his love for surfing, beaches, and trips to the forests of New Zealand. A cousin of his mother also took him on trips to inspect his beehives, an interest that was revived years later when Douglas acquired a few hives of his own.

Though he was shy and self-conscious around adults, Douglas was a gregarious, outgoing teenager who was popular among his peers. At fifteen he dropped out of school and became an apprentice fitter and turner (machinist). His formal education was over, but he continued to be an avid reader. (Many years later he would continue his studies through correspondence school.) Because it was wartime and the company he worked for manufactured war equipment, he worked long hours—six days and three nights a week.

It was also when he was in his teens that he began to wonder about his biological parents. At first his mother was reluctant to give him any information, afraid she would lose her only child. But when she finally agreed to tell him his mother's name, he countered, "No, let me tell you who I think it is," and he named a woman on his paper route. He was right.

"I don't know how I knew she was the one," he reflects now. "She had never done anything to make me think that. I just intuitively figured it out." Occasionally from that point on he discreetly called on his natural mother, who had since married and had other children. These visits became cherished life experiences.

But Jessie Martin's fears of forfeiting her son to his natural mother never became reality; his loyalty to and affection for the parents who raised him never wavered. In fact, only a few years later he strengthened those parental bonds. His adoption had never been finalized because his natural mother had been unwilling to sign the final papers that would irrevocably take away her child. When Douglas was nineteen, he took it on himself to get her signature, file the papers, and pay the fees. At last Martin, the name by which he had been going all his life, was legally his.

After completing a five-year apprenticeship to be a machinist, Douglas worked in Australia for a few months, then returned to New Zealand, where he lived at home and continued his active, outdoor life-style. One evening when he was twenty-three, he was introduced at a dance to Amelia Wati Crawford, a beautiful, dark-haired Maori girl he had admired since he was fourteen, but whom he had never met. As they danced, he asked her to the movies. She accepted — on the condition that he meet her parents first.

The Crawfords were staunch, third-generation Latter-day Saints, and though they were not too pleased that their daughter would be dating a nonmember, they received him warmly and graciously.

The relationship progressed from casual to serious, and Douglas soon became aware of Wati's devotion to the Church. When she told him she wouldn't marry anyone who was not a member, he replied that she could keep going to her church and could raise their children as Mormons. She insisted that wouldn't work, and Douglas was faced with two choices: either quit dating her or see what her church was all about.

As Douglas stepped from the dark, cold winter evening into the brightly lit Mormon chapel, he was immediately made to feel welcome by the all-Maori congregation. He would later comment on the symbolic illumination, for this was a turning point in his life. Wati was the first young woman in New Zealand to receive the Golden Gleaner award of the Young Women's Mutual Improvement Association, and she and her family were well respected by all who knew them. Although much of the meeting was in Maori, which Douglas did not understand, he had an almost overwhelming feeling of warmth and friendship. "I was fellowshipped as well as any person has ever been," he says. He continued to attend meetings with her.

"I already pay taxes, and by the time I pay tithing I won't have much left for myself," he complained to her one evening as they were walking together.

"You'll still have nine-tenths," she replied in her soft, velvet voice.

"I still remember the exact spot where she said that," he recalls. "It was a small thing, but it made a big impression on me. Everything I saw about the Church, I felt good about. I didn't understand much of the doctrine, but I knew I loved her and that she wanted me to be baptized."

Becoming a member of the Church would mean considerable changes in Douglas's life-style. His parents and friends also thought he had "gone off the rails" by becoming involved with a Maori girl—and a Mormon one at that. He was receiving opposition from all sides. "It upset me that I was changing my life for the better, and yet everyone close to me was giving me such a hard time about it. But that just made me dig in my toes and become even more determined to carry on with what I was doing. And, of course," he adds, "I had a profound respect for this young woman.

"As soon as I started investigating the Church, her parents and family and the whole Mormon community were kindness and love themselves. And so, considering what I was giving away, I was thrice blessed by what I was receiving." He was baptized in September 1951 at the age of twenty-four.

Because of the alienation he felt from some with whom he had previously been friendly, Douglas no longer felt comfortable playing rugby on his former team. He was invited to play on the Church's all-Maori senior rugby team, but a lifetime of subtly inbred prejudice and distinctions made him uneasy. So he simply decided not to play that season. But when the coach of the Mormon team came to him and said, "We have paid your rugby dues for the season. Won't you come and play on our team?" — he had an immediate change of attitude. "I suddenly felt very ashamed that I would harbor the least amount of reservations against people who had been so good to me," he says. "It wasn't that I was such a good player, they were just expressing brotherly love for me. So I played as hard as I could for them, even against my former team, and thoroughly enjoyed it."

Now that Douglas was a member of the Church, he and Wati began making wedding plans. Then she was called on a full-time mission as secretary to the manager of Church construction in the Pacific. Away she went with a ring on her finger, much to her fiancé's dismay. "Here I was baptized, engaged, and I wanted to get married. I had given up my old lifestyle and friends and suddenly my lifeline had gone out of town." When he spoke to her parents about it, her father told him how they had always dreamed that Wati would fill a mission. "I quickly learned that what I thought about it didn't count much," he says.

Desperately lonely, he moved to another town and threw himself into his work, determined to save money for their marriage. But after several months he too was called on a mission and his earnings were put to another use. As he began studying and teaching the gospel intensively, the transformation that began with his baptism was more fully realized. The truthfulness of the doctrines began to distill upon his soul (see D&C 121:45), and the firm conviction that would one day sustain him as a General Authority began to congeal in his breast.

Sister Martin spoke of the experience in 1987 in a newspaper interview: "When he began attending Church, I was afraid he was willing to join just to get me to marry him, that the gospel was really secondary. But our mission calls served as a nice test. I soon realized he was genuinely converted to the gospel for all the right reasons." (*Church News*, May 2, 1987, p. 6.)

While he was serving a mission, Douglas came to appreciate the significance of temple marriage. He wrote to Wati and suggested that after their missions they travel by ship to be married in the Hawaiian Temple. Since his savings were depleted when he was released from his mission, Douglas thought he would have to sell his car to finance the trip, but Wati's father offered to pay for the couple's tickets to Hawaii, since they wouldn't be having a wedding reception. Douglas and Wati made the voyage with about twenty other Maoris, including Wati's elderly grandmother and aunt, who were going to receive their own endowments in the temple. They were married on June 2, 1954, three years after becoming engaged.

When the newlyweds returned home three weeks later, they discovered her parents had decided to give them a reception anyway. What a festive occasion it was, with traditional Maori singing and entertainment from the bride's family, combined with Scottish bagpipes and kilts from the groom's family. Once George and Jessie Martin had gotten to know Wati, they "took her to themselves," and wholeheartedly embraced her and the positive changes in their son's life, though they never joined the Church themselves.

For two years the couple remained in Hastings. Then they moved to Hamilton, where the New Zealand Temple was under construction. Douglas became assistant foreman for a small plastics company and was soon called as president of the Hamilton Branch. When the temple was dedicated in April 1958, he was ordained a high priest and set apart as a sealer in the temple by President David O. McKay. He also left the plastics company to work for four years as temple recorder, a full-time, paid position. The first stake outside the United States and Canada was organized in New Zealand in May 1958, and Douglas became bishop of the Hamilton Ward. Later that year he and two other local leaders were the first international visitors invited by the Church to attend general conference.

Elder Martin shakes his head incredulously when he contemplates how the gospel has enriched his life. For example, through the spirit of Elijah, he felt a strong desire to search out his own bloodlines. He discovered he had some younger half brothers and sisters—children of his natural father—and that some of them had also become members of the Church. Through the years he has had many associations with these siblings and has developed strong bonds of love with them and their children, helping to satisfy a childhood desire to be part of a large, close family.

Getting to know his natural father has also been a rare experience for Elder Martin. He found a man with the same kind of expansive, convivial, and forthright personality and a similar love of the outdoors and physical pursuits—someone remarkably like himself, but without benefit of gospel influence. As the two men became better acquainted, his father confessed that he regretted many of the things in his past life.

"When he said that, my feelings toward him changed," explains Elder Martin. "I guess I had been carrying a little bitterness toward him for the part he played—and didn't play—in my life. But then I thought, 'Who knows what kind of life I would have led if I hadn't joined the Church?' I'm glad I found the gospel. The whole thing—temple marriage, gospel, children—just keeps adding more strength. And I needed that strength, maybe more than a lot of people."

But even the advantages of gospel and temple marriage

couldn't guarantee that all of Douglas and Wati's desires for home and family would be fulfilled. For the first ten years of their marriage they were childless, an ironic twist of fate for a man so eager to have his own family around him. Then, in a gesture perhaps difficult to understand outside the Maori culture, Wati's younger sister and her husband, who had a large family of their own, gave two little boys to the Martins to raise. "It was the ultimate expression of love," says Elder Martin. "James was three years old and Sidney was six months." The children brought with them the sense of security and belonging Elder Martin had been seeking all of his life. At last he was really part of a family—his family.

Seven years later the seemingly impossible happened: Wati conceived and delivered a healthy, beautiful baby boy. They named the child Douglas Jonathan—"Douglas after me, and Jonathan meaning 'gift from God,' which he truly was." Two and a half years later came another son, whom they named Craig, Elder Martin's mother's maiden name. "I was over the moon," says Elder Martin. With four little boys, the couple's joy and gratitude to the Lord were boundless.

But a short twenty-two months later, as Elder Martin was on his way to general conference in Salt Lake City, he received word in Hawaii that Craig had drowned. Prior to this, Elder Martin had come to the realization that finally he had tasted a total, utter love—unlike anything he had known before—and that the greatest depth of sorrow he could know would be the loss of a precious family member. But that it could actually happen was unthinkable. Through the intensity of his grief, he discovered a capacity in himself that he hadn't known existed—the ability to have complete love and trust in the Lord. "Though I loved that child as much as any father could love any son, I never asked the Lord 'Why?' I accepted his will without question," he explains. "Craig's death gives greater purpose to our family, to try and get to where one of us has already gone . . . " He pauses, then continues in hushed tones, "Little children go straight to the bosom of the Savior."

For four years Elder Martin served as counselor in the Hamilton New Zealand Stake presidency, and for nine years as stake president. At the age of fifty he was ordained as stake patriarch, and a few months later he was called as regional representative.

In 1962, after working for four years as recorder at the New Zealand Temple, he returned to his job in the plastics company, which eventually grew to be the largest of its type in the country. He was promoted frequently, and when he retired in April 1987, he was the company operations manager. "I advanced in my career beyond a lot of people who had higher degrees and many with more technical skill, because of the training I received by working with people in the Church. I learned how to get along with people in all levels and stations of life, from customers, suppliers, and those on the factory floor right through the executive level. My Church service has also taught me how to make decisions, something many people have trouble with. I was promoted because of those skills."

Although Elder Martin dropped out of school at age fifteen, he has always had the ambition to continue to progress and improve himself. In his mid-thirties he began studies in management through correspondence school. When he completed the first year of course work—despite the added pressures of job, Church, and family—he was astonished to learn that he had received the top marks in the country—"my one and only academic achievement," he says, smiling.

His smile, genuine and infectious, wreathes his hazel eyes with good-natured laugh lines. He has white hair and a tall, robust stature with an easy grace that, despite a recent broken back, bespeaks a lifetime of physical activities. The injury occurred the last time he indulged in body surfing on a warm day during the 1986 Christmas holidays, summertime in New Zealand. He and his son were far from shore when he was caught in a broken wave that tossed him around and rammed his head into the ocean floor. Knowing something was very wrong, he dragged himself onto the beach, where he waited, stunned, for his son. Later, when he admitted to the ambulance driver that perhaps he should start acting his age, fifty-nine, the man shrugged and commented, "It's better to burn out than rust out."

Elder Martin has done neither, though he hasn't been surfing since he was sustained as a member of the First Quorum of the Seventy in April 1987. For his fellow New Zealanders, his calling as the first native New Zealander General Authority is a significant milestone, for, as one writer observes, "he represents many New Zealand priesthood leaders who, like him, have served as bishops, stake presidents, temple sealers, and regional representatives. He symbolizes the status and maturity of the restored Church in New Zealand." (R. Lanier Britsch, "Roots of Faith," *Ensign*, September 1989, p. 50.)

Elder Martin's first assignment in this calling was second counselor to the president of the Philippines/Micronesia/Guam in the North Pacific Area, and a year later he was called to the same position for the Pacific Area, which includes everything between the African and South American continents below the equator. For this assignment, he and Sister Martin relocated to Sydney, Australia. In October 1989 he was called as first counselor of that area. Covering such a wide area keeps the Martins on the move, but they are in good health and bounce back quickly from the stress of frequent travel and time changes.

In May 1989, when Elder Martin visited an eye specialist for what he believed was an abrasion on the surface of his

156

right eye, he was told he had a malignancy, one that rarely appears in the eye, which could be fatal if left unchecked. That diagnosis was confirmed by a second specialist. In a three-and-a-half hour operation a few days later, the malignancy was removed, taking with it a crescent-shaped piece of his cornea half the size of a penny. Although the situation was worrisome for Elder Martin and his family, he was told in a blessing shortly before the surgery that the treatment would be successful, and neither his eyesight, his health, nor his service to the Lord would be adversely affected. The cornea transplant was successful, and within months his vision was as good as it had been before the incident.

Since becoming a General Authority, Elder Martin has been especially impressed by the dedication he has seen in missionaries, especially the older missionary couples. He spoke of this in his first general conference address. "Whenever I meet and talk with missionary couples, I am filled with love and respect for their humility and desire to help the Filipino Saints. They regard their missions as one of the great opportunities to serve the Master in their lives. They always ask, 'How many grandchildren have you?' Our response of eight is quickly overshadowed with 'We have sixteen,' or 'twenty-three,' or maybe 'twenty-seven,' and almost always with 'And there are two we haven't seen yet.' They miss their family and grandchildren, but don't complain. Instead, they look forward to that great homecoming reunion. Meanwhile, they are given all the love they can absorb from devoted Filipino Saints." (*Ensign*, November 1987, p. 24.)

This attitude of respect extends to the Brethren with whom he serves in the First and Second Quorums of the Seventy. Although it could be argued that there is no "typical" General Authority, Elder Martin's upbringing and experiences certainly deviate from the perceived profile. "When I look at myself and my background, and then look around me at the men I serve with—men of great accomplishment and education, university graduates and highly successful professionals—I consider myself the least of them," he says with characteristic self-effacement. "Maybe I feel a bit of the shy, insecure kid I used to be, but that doesn't stop me from having the confidence to go forth and do what the Lord requires of me now."

Humility and faith born of obedience and commitment, not an inspiring record of scholarly degrees and worldly feats, are what the Lord expects of his servants. By this standard, Elder Martin's qualifications are abundant. As he strives to model his behavior after the perfect example set by the Savior, he seeks to win approval not of the world, but of the Lord.

ALEXANDER B. MORRISON

Alexander B. Morrison is a scholar, a scientist, and an administrator—one who speaks with the confidence and fluency born of knowledge, education, and years of being in the public eye. There is a forthright directness about him that says here is a man people listen to and believe.

But when he talks of things close to his heart, his voice trembles and his eyes become moist. At times his words are slow and deliberate as he searches for the right phrase to express his innermost feelings. Other times, he never waxes more eloquent than when he is filled with the Spirit of the Lord and moved by compassion and love for his fellow beings. For this is a man full of contradictions. He was born into the most humble home, yet he has achieved high-level government positions and international recognition. He is an intellectual who is comfortable associating with some of the world's most brilliant persons, yet he feels an equality of brotherhood among the world's most poor and illiterate. He has earned the acclaim and gratitude of national leaders, yet he is a humble servant who obeys the Lord's anointed without question or hesitation.

Elder Morrison has devoted many years of his life to fighting malnutrition and disease. Before being called as a member of the First Quorum of the Seventy in April 1987, and a member of the Second Quorum two years later, he served as an advisor to many committees of the World Health Organization (WHO), an agency of the United Nations dedicated to improving the health of people everywhere, but primarily in third-world countries. In this capacity he visited Africa many times and fell under the spell of the huge continent. "There's something about Africa which, for some people, becomes a life-long love affair," he claims. "Once it's got its hooks into you, you can't get away. I've been hooked, and it has affected my life profoundly."

For several years Elder Morrison chaired the Scientific and Technical Advisory Committee to WHO's Special Program for Research and Training in Tropical Diseases. The job of this committee was to combat such diseases as malaria, leprosy, sleeping sickness, and onchocerciasis, or river blindness, a parasitic disease spread by a black fly that flourishes in the Volta River Basin area of West Africa. Every year many thousands, mostly children, were blinded by the disease. Elder Morrison was involved in the development and distribution of Ivermectin, a drug that today promises virtually to eliminate this scourge. "For seven years now [in 1990], as a result of extensive spraying programs to kill black flies that spread the disease, now supplemented by the availability of Ivermectin, there have been no more people blinded," he reports.

In addition to his work in Africa with WHO, Elder Morrison's first assignment as a General Authority was as second counselor to the president of the United Kingdom/Ireland/ Africa Area. He finds it impossible to separate his secular from his religious interests in the more than 400 million black Africans, which gives him a unique dual perspective. His expertise as a scientist, with degrees in nutrition and pharmacology, is enriched immeasurably by his knowledge of the gospel. "My perspective gives me a greatly enhanced sense of brotherhood and obligation, as well as a realization of the changes that can come into these people's lives through the gospel of Christ," he explains. This sensitivity to the suffering and deprivation he has seen has become a burden he carries with him constantly.

"I remember what starvation looks like as I sit down to abundance three times a day," he says. "I feel jungle heat on my skin as I move through air-conditioned corridors. I carry victims' faces in my mind as I brush my teeth and rinse my mouth with water whose purity I take for granted."

Elder Morrison believes that many Latter-day Sants have some misconceptions about the African people—that the Africans are "ignorant, illiterate, woolly-headed savages with no history and nothing to commend them," and that they have somehow brought their horrible circumstances on themselves. This is simply not the case. Rather, they are intelligent and courageous with a fundamental understanding of the importance of families. "If one works, a dozen eat," he points out.

"You cannot help but feel the fear and worry an African father has. He loves his children, just as we love ours, and he knows malaria will be back in the wet season and some of his children will probably die," he said in a *Church News* interview. "And if the rains don't come, he knows there will be no food. I was in a village two years ago and the rains were three weeks late. Those poor people had to decide whether to plant the last seed grain they had or to eat it. That was a sad village with slack-eyed women, pot-bellied children and gaunt men. They live on the brink of disaster all the time. They had the courage to plant. How many of us could do that?" (*Church News*, May 10, 1987, p. 14.)

Tears fill his eyes as he describes the heart-breaking conditions he has witnessed, poverty so wretched that "you can't imagine what it's like unless you've seen it, destitution ten times worse than anything we have in this country." Some people view the widespread poverty and affliction as a contradiction of the existence of God, or at least of a caring, concerned Heavenly Father. But not Elder Morrison. "God is not the author of such injustice and tragedy. He weeps at what he sees more than do I—and I do weep for the children. But these conditions are the products of ignorance, greed, and selfishness. The answer to the devastation these people suffer is the gospel of Jesus Christ."

At last the time is at hand for the "dawning of a brighter day," as the gospel spreads throughout Africa, said Elder Morrison, speaking in general conference shortly after being called as a Seventy. "The light of the fulness of the gospel of Christ, like a beam of transcendent clarity and effulgent beauty, is bursting majestic upon those ancient lands and peoples. It dispels the spiritual gloom and drives away the shadows of error and superstition which long have lain over the 'dark continent.' It falls on a prepared people—a people prepared by the Spirit of God. . . . If the price of spirituality be suffering and affliction, travail and sorrow, our humble African brothers and sisters are well prepared to receive and obey the fulness of the gospel of Christ." (*Ensign*, November 1987, p. 25.)

"When they become converted to the gospel, the scales of ignorance and superstition fall away and they raise themselves up," he explains. A common mistake of charitable groups is to make those they help become dependent. "The

Mormon way is to teach them to look after themselves and then stand back and let them do it—teach them to grow their own grain instead of depending on handouts of grain. All of the African converts I've ever known have had their lives improved, some dramatically, by the living gospel."

One such person is a physician in eastern Nigeria. Like many other African men, he drank a lot and was abusive to his wife and their children. "When he heard about the gospel he went to his wife in tears, which is difficult for an African man to do, because it is considered unmanly to treat a woman as anything but chattel," relates Elder Morrison. "But he did, and he told her, 'From this day forth I promise I will never again be unfaithful to you; I will not stay out at night drinking; I will not beat you and I will be a good father.' About a year later his wife, who was an educated woman herself with a degree in political science, told me, 'Elder Morrison, he has been true to his word, I have a real man now.' And he *is* a real man now, a leader in the Church with a strong testimony of the truth. Only the gospel in its broadest sense has the power to touch men's hearts like that. And only the gospel can touch our hearts and make us sensitive to the suffering of our brothers and sisters."

Perhaps it was the humbleness of Elder Morrison's own beginnings that drew him into a life of service to the poor and underprivileged. He was born the middle of five children on a "very, very modest farm" in the prairies of northcentral Alberta, Canada. "I was an impoverished farm kid who went barefoot all summer and got one pair of overalls and a shirt in the fall." His paternal grandfather was John Morrison, a Scottish laborer and coal miner who never learned to read or write but who had a cherished ambition to improve his lot. In 1911, at age fifty-three, he took his family from Scotland to Canada, where land was cheap and plentiful. Conditions in northern Alberta were harsh and unyielding, as was the living the family eked out, but they adapted and survived. His mother's family also came from Scotland in the early 1900s, when his mother was a "wee girl of eight or nine," and settled in the same untamed land of central Alberta, four miles from their nearest neighbor and twenty miles from town.

"That makes me straight Scots," says Elder Morrison. "When I go back I'm taken back into the language of my childhood within half a sentence. I'm at hoome thaire because I'm one a' their ain lads, ye ken, noot a fooreigner," he says, lapsing into a Scottish brogue.

His parents, Alexander S. and Christina Wilson Morrison, settled in Vermilion, 125 miles east of Edmonton, Alberta. They taught their five children to worship God and work hard, the latter a quality Alexander didn't much appreciate at the time, but for which he is very grateful now. Many of the never-ending chores that abound in farm life fell to him, the middle child. He began his education at age five in a one-room schoolhouse two miles from home. During the bitterly cold winters, swathed from head to toe, he followed in his older brothers' tracks, his own legs too short to break a trail in the deep drifts as they trudged to school.

"There are two kinds of Scots; one type is wild, stubborn, and proud, and the other sweet, compassionate, and truly Christian," claims Elder Morrison. "My mother's people were the second type, and certainly she was the great gentling influence in my life. If ever I was hurt as a wee lad, I would run and bury my face in her apron. I still remember the way her apron smelled—like bread, warm and comforting like my mother."

His father was the first type, with a quick temper and prickly pride. Yet, despite his flaws, he taught his children three things: to be honest, to honor integrity ("if you gave your word about something you had to keep it"), and to love learning. In the small farming community, where little premium was placed on education, he always provided books for his children and saw to it that they finished high school, which Alex thought was of "monstrous size—eighty-seven students and four rooms." Alex didn't plan to continue his education; no one in his family had ever gone to a university, and he assumed he would go into farming, although "I was always kind of clumsy on the farm and not very well suited to it," he admits.

However, his father, who had been apprenticed to a baker at the age of fourteen and always regretted his lack of formal education, told his son in no uncertain terms, "You are brighter than you think you are, and you have an obligation to develop your mind." All Alex needed was that one little push into educational waters, where he quickly discovered he loved to swim, and the University of Alberta became his wide ocean. As soon as he adjusted to city life—Edmonton, with a population of 95,000, was the largest city in the province—he dove into academia with all the vigor his eager, untried soul could muster. That year, 1947, thousands of homecoming soldiers, anxious to catch up their lives after World War II, swelled the classrooms and toughened the competition. But the farmboy rose to the challenge and graduated at the top of his class with a bachelor's degree in agriculture and then a master's in nutrition. He was fascinated by the blend of scientific areas a major in nutrition offered—biochemistry, medicine, agriculture, anthropology, and sociology—and by graduation he was a devoted scientist.

His university years brought a spiritual as well as an educational awakening. David Blackmore, a humble, serious World War II veteran, told his younger classmate about his church, The Church of Jesus Christ of Latter-day Saints, and gave him copies of the books *Articles of Faith* and *Jesus the Christ* by James E. Talmage. Alex was immediately convinced

of the truthfulness of what he read, and was especially interested in two doctrines. The first was that we are put on
this earth to learn. To a university student hooked on the
wonders of education, being told that the glory of God is
intelligence, and that he, as a son of that omniscient being,
has the possibility of learning and progressing eternally, was
very appealing. Second, the principle of eternal marriage was
especially attractive. He was dating Shirley Brooks—"the
most beautiful girl I had ever met in my whole life; the only
girl I ever went out with or ever wanted to go out with, and
the only one I ever dated or kissed that I wasn't related to."
The thought of being sealed to her forever was almost too
splendid to be believed. When Shirley read the same materials
and was equally convinced they were true, the couple were
baptized in December 1950. He was twenty and she was
seventeen. N. Eldon Tanner was their first branch president,
and Hugh B. Brown was their Sunday School teacher. Both
of these men would later serve as General Authorities.

Alex met Shirley at the university farm, of which her father
was the superintendent. He was drawn to the five-foot-two
high school student with the blue eyes, brown hair, and pretty
face—"Oh, dear me, she was beautiful!" he interjects. But he
was even more attracted to the great reservoir of goodness
he felt in her. They became best friends right away, talking
incessantly and missing each other immensely when apart,
and they still feel the same way forty years later. A week after
they were baptized, they were married, and later they were
sealed in the Alberta Temple.

After Alex completed his master's degree in 1952, he took
a government job in Ottawa for a year. Then he moved to
Ithaca, New York, to attend Cornell University, and earned
his Ph.D. in 1956. The years in New York were happy ones
for the Morrisons, though they were "as poor as the proverbial
church mice," struggling to make it by on a monthly stipend

of $207. Alex worked fourteen hours a day, six days a week, at the university, and Shirley worked just as hard at home, caring for the children who came along right away (they had three by the time they left Ithaca, and five more were born over the next few years).

After graduation, Alex worked three years in the nutritional research department of a pharmaceutical company in Evansville, Indiana, studying ways to improve infant formula, among other projects. He also became president of the Evansville Branch of the Church. In 1959 he took his family back to Ottawa, where he took a drastic cut in order to work as a research chemist for the Food and Drug Directorate, the national agency that controls the quality of food and drugs in Canada. Soon he was again made branch president, and Shirley was active in Relief Society and the Young Women's Mutual Improvement Association.

In 1966 the Canadian government asked Alex to return to school for a master's degree in pharmacology. So the Morrisons moved again, this time to the University of Michigan, where Alex was now one of the older students, competing against younger ones. "These kids aren't going to beat me," he determined, and once again he graduated number one in his class.

Then it was back to his government post in Canada, and in 1971 he was named assistant deputy minister over the Health Protection Branch, the Canadian agency charged with regulating food, drugs, cosmetics, medical devices, pesticides, harmful radiation, and dangerous chemicals and microorganisms. In that capacity, he held the highest-ranking nonelected government position ever held in Canada by a Mormon. For the thirteen years he ran that agency, he supervised a $110 million annual budget and 2,000 employees, made approximately 25,000 regulatory decisions yearly, had two full-time press secretaries, and appeared almost daily in the press or on television. He learned to make high-pressure decisions quickly, decisions sometimes worth billions of dollars, and became fascinated by the interface between science and public policy. Under his direction the organization became known as one of the best regulatory agencies in the world. However, Elder Morrison was even more satisfied with its reputation for honesty, a standard that must run from top to bottom in any organization, depending heavily on the ethics of its leader. Because of the nature of the business, opportunities for dishonesty were abundant. "If we were to let a drug go on the market before everything was right, or were willing to wink at some malfeasance, there were possibilities to make a lot of crooked money fast," he explains.

Several years after Elder Morrison retired, his son Allen met one of his father's former colleagues, who told the younger Morrison, "The thing I remember most about your dad is his integrity."

"If I am to be remembered for anything, I would rather it be for honesty," Elder Morrison says.

Burned out after many years of such a high-pressure, high-visibility job, Dr. Morrison retired from public service in 1984 and took a position as a professor and chairman of the Food Science Department at the University of Guelph, near Toronto. Even during the times he was busiest professionally, he was active in the Church, serving as bishop, stake high councilor, and in several district and branch presidencies. He admits that he didn't always have as much time to spend with his children as he would have liked. But now his life slowed considerably and he was able to concentrate more on Church and family, as well as teaching and consulting.

He also had more time to devote to the World Health Organization, with which he had been involved since the early 1970s. In 1981 he had taken a sabbatical from government service to serve as a consultant to the director general of the WHO in Geneva, Switzerland. As a result of this association, he earned a reputation as a fighter of tropical diseases and developed his consuming passion for Africa. In 1984 he became the first recipient of the David M. Kennedy International Service Award from the Kennedy International Center at Brigham Young University, in recognition of his international efforts to improve health and nutrition.

On March 24, 1987, Dr. Morrison was on a WHO assignment in Geneva when the phone rang in his hotel room. A voice came on the line and asked, in English, "Is this Elder Morrison?" When he confirmed that it was, he was asked to hold for President Thomas S. Monson. Elder Morrison, who was serving as a regional representative for Eastern Canada at that time, had met President Monson nearly thirty years before, when President Monson served as a mission president in Canada. After the two friends talked for a while, President Monson told Elder Morrison he was being called as a member of the First Quorum of the Seventy. Then he asked, "Would that be convenient for you?"

"I told him it may not be convenient, but that wasn't the point. My wife and I made the decision many years before to serve the Lord in any way he required of us."

The Morrisons immediately began preparing their lives to answer the Lord's call. "We had three months to tear up all of the roots we had put down in the last thirty-five years," he recalls. "I resigned at the university and we sold our home, cars, and many other things and put the rest of our belongings in storage. I quit all of the consulting and committee work I had been doing and severed all ties with the WHO. Since then, although I have many fond memories of the people and places I've known and things I've done, I have not had a single moment of regret or doubt. When the Lord calls you, that's the end of the game for everything else. If you look back, you're not fit to be a servant. Besides that," he adds, "I have a special love for President Monson. If he had asked me to jump out the hotel window, I might have hesitated for half a moment on the ledge, but not any more than that."

The call did not take the Morrisons completely unawares, for they had felt for several months that something was coming that would change their lives. At first Elder Morrison felt as if he were an unlikely person to be serving among the brethren. "There was probably no greater stranger among the General Authorities than I," he claims. "I was nobody's relation, nobody's friend. I didn't go to school with any of them and had met only two or three members of the Twelve. But although I came in as a stranger, they have made me feel like a brother."

Having spent most of his life in highly competitive situations, replete with all of the backstabbing and corruption such positions have to offer, he very much appreciates the differences he now finds among his colleagues. "Here is a group of men who are as diverse as mankind itself, yet I am touched by the brotherhood and loving concern I feel among them. The love the brethren have for President Benson and each other is a real example of how we should all treat one another. It is certainly a contrast to what you find out in the world."

In his assignment as first counselor to the president of the United Kingdom/Ireland/Africa Area, Elder and Sister Morrison were headquartered in Solihull, West Midlands, England. Only Mary, the youngest of their eight children, was living with them. The others were all pursuing studies or careers: Heather as a student at Brigham Young University; Jeffrey, attending law school in Toronto; Allen John, a business professor at the University of Western Ontario; Sandra, a homemaker in Toronto; Howard, a graduate student at the University of North Carolina; Barbara, a homemaker in Edmonton; and David, an archeologist with the Canadian National Museum in Ottawa.

For Elder Morrison, the transition from scientist-administrator to General Authority has come fairly easily, but has also brought with it increased sensitivity to the frailties of man, including his own. He has, he believes, become more patient, more tolerant. He now has more time to spend with his eternal companion, Shirley, as they labor side by side in the Lord's vineyard. "The great blessing in my life is that my wife is such a superb woman and such a superb mother," he says. "I am married to an angel."

Though his Church assignments require a lot of administrative duties and "paper pushing," Elder Morrison is an experienced manager who is used to handling the organizational mechanics decisively and efficiently, leaving him as much time as possible for people. On a recent afternoon, after hours spent making phone calls, writing letters, and finishing up other details, he spent an hour counseling with a friend who had fallen away from the Church. He gave the man a blessing and the two wept together. Later a woman came to his office to discuss having her blessings restored following disciplinary action, a "tender, tender time when many more tears were shed," he says. "That's when I realized that that is what the work amounts to—you have to do the administration, but it is the ministering that really counts. There are plenty of opportunities for both."

Although Elder Morrison's calling as a member of the Second Quorum of the Seventy is probably a temporary one (members of that quorum generally serve for five years), he is not concerned about what the future holds. Once released from full-time Church service, he may go back to teaching in a university, perhaps in Canada or at BYU. He and Sister Morrison would like to be near their children and grandchildren, if possible, and would like to do temple work. He has recently completed a book on the Church in Black Africa, *The Dawning of a Brighter Day* (Salt Lake City: Deseret Book, 1990). He enjoys writing, having published volumes of scholarly articles, and will probably continue in that pursuit as well.

Elder Morrison has always that found his profound religious convictions have reinforced his stature and knowledge as a scientist. "I've never encountered anything but the greatest respect from my non-Mormon professional associates," he declares. "I think there is a considerable respect for someone who believes in something. Besides, how could there ever be a conflict? Wherever there appears to be one, you can be sure the revealed religion is correct, and the scientists will just have to go back and rethink their position. Christ knows more chemistry than I'll ever know, at least in this life. 'Truth is truth where e'er 'tis found, whether on Christian or on heathen ground,' " he quotes.

It is difficult to imagine any future for Elder Morrison in which he is not involved, at least on some level, with Africa. In 1987 he accompanied Elder Marvin J. Ashton of the Council of the Twelve to that continent for the dedication of three countries for the preaching of the gospel, and in the spring of 1990 he assisted Elder Neal A. Maxwell in dedicating two more lands. These nations, together with the other countries where proselyting is already taking place, are fulfilling the prophecy that the gospel will be carried "unto the uttermost part of the earth" (Acts 1:8), says Elder Morrison.

"The bursting of the gospel light upon Africa is a great manifestation and testimony of God's love for all of his children. . . . The gleaning and gathering of the children of God in Africa is just beginning. In the words of the Prophet Joseph Smith, 'it will go forward . . . till the purposes of God shall be accomplished, and the Great Jehovah shall say the work is done' (*History of the Church,* 4:540)." (*Ensign,* November 1987, p. 26.)

This work of spreading the gospel and becoming as one with our brothers and sisters of the world is a responsibility that must necessarily involve every member of the Church, according to Elder Morrison. He refers to the twenty-fifth chapter of Matthew in which the Lord charges all of his followers with feeding the hungry and ministering to the sick. "We can't all go to Africa to help dig wells or nurse dying children, nor can we all go on welfare missions. But each of us can be more loving and tolerant. We can eliminate the prejudice and bigotry from our own souls, realizing that we truly are a global family."

ROBERT E. SACKLEY

The message was concise and cryptic: "If you are ever at the University of Nigeria, please drop in on Dr. Ike Ikeme, a professor in the Food Science Department." There was no explanation, and neither the unfamiliar signature nor the United States postmark bore any other clues.

To Robert E. Sackley, president of the Nigeria Lagos Mission, the note piqued his curiosity and gave him a vague, unexplained sensation of promise and anticipation. Who was Ike Ikeme? He had no record of any Church members in Nsukka, where the university was located. That area of Africa had never been opened up for proselyting, and the branch closest to that city was more than four hours away by car.

President Sackley's attention was already divided between two mission homes in the burgeoning mission — one in Lagos and the other in the eastern Nigerian city of Aba —

and heavy responsibilities more than occupied his time. How much credence should he give to a mysterious note from someone he didn't know?

Yet, try as he might, he couldn't get the matter out of his mind. A few months later he had some business in a city near Nsukka, and he soon found himself, with his wife and another missionary couple, at the Food Science Department on the University of Nigeria campus.

"School is on summer recess now," he was told. "Dr. Ikeme is not only away from the university, he is out of town on vacation." President Sackley turned to leave just as a man came out of another office. The man explained that he was on the faculty with Dr. Ikeme, and that Dr. Ikeme had returned to town the night before. The two professors lived near one another, and he offered to take President Sackley to Dr. Ikeme's home.

As President Sackley pulled up at a well-kept but modest home, a fine-looking Igbo (an African tribe) man walked out of the front door and approached the car.

"Hello, president, how are you?" the man said.

Taken aback, the mission president asked, "How do you know who I am?"

"For six and a half years I have been praying that you would come," was the response. "For the last few days I have felt that your visit was imminent."

Dr. Ikeme introduced himself and invited the visitors into his home, where they met his family, a beautiful woman and three small children.

President Sackley could contain his curiosity no longer. "Dr. Ikeme, what is your connection with the Mormon church?"

"I am a Mormon, a very committed one," he said. "And one who has been waiting for you for a very long time."

He went on to explain that he had attended Purdue University in Indiana, where he had met two sister missionaries from Salt Lake City. "Although I was a tough contact, they finally convinced me of the truthfulness of the gospel. When I completed my Ph.D. in 1981, I was endowed in the Salt Lake Temple before returning home." Dr. Ikeme had been told not to do any missionary work in Nigeria until the missionaries came and the work could be commenced properly. Devoutly obedient, he had kept that counsel and had never spoken about the Church, even to his wife, whom he had met and married shortly after returning to his homeland.

Patience Ikeme was from a family of devout members of the Church of England and wanted to marry a fellow Christian. When her fiancé responded to her questions that he was not only a Christian, but a Mormon as well, she asked, "What is a Mormon?"

He uttered the line that was to become the byword for their next several years together: "You just watch me."

Now President Sackley turned to Patience, an educated woman who was completing a master's degree, and asked, "After six years of marriage and three children, what do you know about the Mormon church?"

"I know nothing about it except that it is true."

"How could you know the Church is true when you know nothing about it?" he asked.

"It is true because my man is true," was her simple reply. "He would never belong to anything that wasn't right."

Dr. Ikeme had kept his commitment not to teach the gospel, and at last, after six long years, he became an eager participant as President Sackley began giving the missionary discussions to Patience. She was baptized not long after that, and a few months later Dr. Ikeme became President Ikeme of the Nsukka Branch, and Sister Ikeme became president of the branch Relief Society. A short time later Dr. Ikeme was called as the president of the Enugu District.

"Nsukka will someday make a great ward of the Enugu Stake," Dr. Ikeme was told recently.

"No, *Enugu* will make a great ward of the *Nsukka* Stake," he replied with a grin.

Brother and Sister Ikeme are just two of many persons who have touched and been touched by Elder Sackley's resolute testimony and humble resolve to do the work of the Lord. Since his conversion more than forty years ago, this five-foot eight-inch former soldier has firmly believed that all peoples will eventually have the chance to hear the gospel. He has accepted a personal challenge to take that opportunity to as many as he can. This quest has taken him from his boyhood home in Australia around the world to Canada, to Church assignments in Salt Lake City and Washington, D.C., to mission presidencies in the Philippines and Nigeria, and, most recently, to an assignment as counselor to the president of the British Isles/Ireland/Africa Area. One friend estimates that Elder Sackley has personally brought more than 125 converts into the Church. And as his areas of responsibility have widened, who knows how many countless others have in some way been influenced by his love of the gospel, and his missionary efforts?

Born in 1922 in Lismore, New South Wales, Australia, Robert Sackley credits his "goodly parents," Cecil James and Mary Isabel Duncan Sackley, with his membership in the Church. Though they weren't members, their teachings of right and wrong, and their high personal code of conduct, enabled him to recognize and accept the truth when he heard it. His father, he says, was "an absolutely moral man who was devoutly committed" to his wife and children. A veterinarian whose love of animals and training of cattle dogs was legendary, Cecil was a hero of the Australian armed forces in the World War I battle of Gallipoli, Turkey. As a result of contacting nerve gas while fighting in France, he suffered permanent lung damage, which plagued him the rest of his life and eventually caused his death at the age of sixty.

Both parents were Episcopalians, but it was Mary Sackley who took her religion to heart, imbuing her two sons and daughter with a love of God and the desire to pray. A loving, yet precise and exacting woman, she too was troubled by chronic health problems, and when her children were still very young, she was forced to spend twelve months in the hospital. It was a difficult time for the family—made more so by the depression years—but they learned to care for one another and grew closer as a result. As her health improved, she was a tireless worker, and during World War II she served as a volunteer registered nurse for fifty hours a week for six years, never receiving a penny in compensation.

Robert enlisted in the Australian army in World War II and was chosen to serve in the elite commando forces. Members of the unit, which was similar to the Green Berets of the United States, were required to pass rigorous physical and psychological standards, demonstrate the ability to function well in combat, and adhere to high ethical and professional standards. The commandoes were given the most difficult, dangerous tasks, and the mortality rate was high. Asked why he would want to belong to such a unit, Robert replied, "Because when I had the chance to sleep at night, I knew those on guard were always awake," alluding to the integrity of the special forces.

On Christmas Day 1944 an incident occurred that would almost cost him his life and set off a chain of events that irrevocably changed the course of his future. While on a raiding party in New Guinea in the Solomon Islands, thirty miles behind enemy lines, members of the unit were surprised by an enemy ambush. Most of the men were killed, and Robert, already suffering from malaria, was severely wounded, shot in the arm and back. Though covered with blood and trembling with fear and pain, he was forced to lie immobile for several hours, for the slightest movement brought increased machine-gun fire. Toward evening, a familiar voice told him to wait until dark and then somehow make it into the river, where men were waiting about two hundred yards downstream to fish him out.

That night, weak from pain and the loss of blood, Commando Sackley crawled the fifteen yards to the river, rolled over the embankment, and plunged fifteen feet into the water. A brief, treacherous trip down the Puriata River, one of the fastest flowing rivers on earth, whisked him under the nose of the enemy machine gun and to help downstream.

"It was almost better to be killed than wounded," says Elder Sackley, "because we were a raiding party and didn't have a base camp. If you couldn't move out with your unit, you might be left stranded in the jungle." But his commander assigned five sturdy kanakas, or native tribesmen ("We called them the fuzzy, wuzzy angels because of their long black hair," Elder Sackley interjects), to carry him to the nearest U.S. base camp thirty miles away. Hiding from enemy fire by day and picking their way through the jungle by night, the trip took five days.

From the American camp he was transported by ship and then train to an Australian hospital. He was assigned to a hospital in New South Wales, his home state, but he asked to be sent to Queensland instead. "I know now why I made the request, though I was baffled at the time," he says. "I didn't know a soul in Queensland."

When he returned to Australian soil, he did not contact his parents immediately, wanting to wait until his condition was more promising. One day a nurse told him his mother was trying to find him. When he phoned home, his mother explained that a picture of him disembarking from the hospital ship had been published in the newspaper, identified only with the caption "Wounded Australian veteran coming home." With a magnifying glass his parents had identified the grainy picture of their son by reading his military number from his uniform. Since then, Mary Sackley had been searching every hospital in the country. She came immediately to his bedside, and her son was surprised at her appearance, for, he said, "I had left a black-haired mother and five years later came home to a gray-haired old woman." The war experiences of her sons and son-in-law, all of whom had been wounded, had aged her considerably.

At the hospital Robert's back healed and his malaria was under control, but his left arm was not healing. The nerves extending down the forearm had been severed, the bone shattered, and the wound had become gangrenous. At the hospital was a brilliant surgeon who specialized in limb repairs, and shortly after arriving in Queensland, Robert signed the papers giving the surgeon permission to amputate the arm.

While Robert was sitting on the hospital veranda one afternoon, passing time until his strength was built up enough for the surgery, two pretty young women passed by.

"Hello," said the young soldier. ("I have been grateful ever since that I am an extrovert," he says now with a smile.) He soon struck up a friendship with Marjorie Orth, one of the young women, who made it very plain she was a Mormon. She invited him to go to church with her on Sunday, and he was able to arrange a hospital pass. His presence at the meeting, dressed in his commando uniform covered with military decorations, created a stir in a branch that hadn't had a convert since the beginning of the war.

Marjorie also invited him home, where he met her family. After determining that the young man had a great deal of faith in God, John Orth, Marjorie's father and president of the Brisbane Branch, asked if he might give Robert a blessing the night before his operation. In the blessing, President Orth

180

promised him that the surgeon would be prompted not to cut off the limb. Robert, believing amputation was the only solution, didn't put much stock in these words.

When he regained consciousness the following afternoon, after many hours in surgery, he was furious to find that his arm was indeed still there, strapped tightly across his chest and throbbing painfully. "You've left me with a useless arm!" he yelled at the surgeon. "You told me yourself it will never heal!"

"When we were preparing to cut off your arm, I felt that maybe we should give it a little longer to heal," the surgeon explained. He had wired the bones and tried to repair the nerves.

For the next eighteen months Robert underwent intensive therapy. It was a year before any feeling or movement returned to his fingers. Today, although he cannot straighten the arm completely and has slightly diminished capacity in his hand, a white-ridged scar around his elbow is the only reminder that his arm, torn asunder by enemy fire, was saved by the hands of a skilled surgeon and a blessing of faith. "As I look back on it now I am very aware of how the Lord blessed me, although I didn't realize it at the time," recalls Elder Sackley. Although the blessing was not significant to his conversion, Marjorie and her family were.

Impressed with the young man, Marjorie's mother gave him a card containing the Articles of Faith. "You're an intelligent fellow," she told him. "Read these and tell me what you think." He was so impressed by what he read on the card that he memorized all thirteen articles that evening. "From that night to now, I can still say them all by heart," he says. "I don't think most members of the Church realize what a masterpiece they are."

Sister Orth next gave him a copy of the Book of Mormon, which he read completely within the next thirty-six hours.

He instantly recognized its truthfulness and knew there was nothing he could do but be baptized.

"My life was changed . . . as I read the Book of Mormon," Elder Sackley said, speaking of the incident in general conference shortly after he was sustained as a General Authority. "There is nothing on earth that has influenced me more profoundly than my testimony of this sacred record and the work to which it belongs. It has burned within my soul over the years with ever-increasing brightness, and I find great joy and satisfaction in walking in 'newness of life' in my search for the 'more excellent way.' " (*Ensign*, November 1988, p. 22.)

Robert E. Sackley was baptized on June 16, 1946. His mother was heartbroken by what she considered her son's rejection of his childhood teachings and denial of her own religious faith. "I had many hesitations about joining the Church because I felt I was betraying my family," explains Elder Sackley. "I called my father from the military hospital and told him of my decision to be baptized. I have a deep sense of gratitude to a father who simply said, 'I have taught you all I could about right and wrong, morality and purity. If you feel it is right, do it. I trust you.' He helped calm my mother's troubled heart, though she remained bitter against the Church for several years."

Ten months later, on March 26, 1947, Robert and Marjorie were married in a ceremony performed by her father. Robert took a job as a forestry officer, and the young couple moved to a station 160 miles away from the nearest branch of the Church. They had little money, and they could make the long drive over a mountainous road only every few months, so they held Sunday services in their home. But they didn't like the isolation from other Latter-day Saints, and so, without other job prospects and against the advice of colleagues who warned him against so "foolish a move," Robert quit his job and the couple moved to Brisbane. There he soon found work as a tax accountant.

In Brisbane the Sackleys purchased a home for their little family, which now included two daughters, Carolyn and Jennifer. As each child was born and on many other occasions, Mary Sackley visited in her son's home. The bitterness began to go away and she gradually grew to love her granddaughters and daughter-in-law. On one visit her son persuaded her to read *Jesus the Christ* by James E. Talmage. She told him it was the most marvelous book she had ever read, and she wanted to investigate the Church. However, within days she became very ill and was admitted to the hospital for surgery, her fourth operation in four years. She did not survive the surgery. Not long after that, Cecil Sackley suffered a collapsed lung and died as well.

Losing both his parents in such a short time reminded Robert and Marjorie of the importance of their eternal family and the Lord's plan of salvation. Once again, devotion to the Lord motivated them to leave everything behind and move again, this time to be near a temple where they could be sealed and do his parents' temple work as well. They investigated the possibility of going to the United States, but there was a twelve-year waiting list for Australians to get U.S. work visas, so they decided to go to Cardston, Alberta, Canada. Because they couldn't afford round-trip fares, they planned to work for a year before returning home.

Coincidentally, the ship they boarded in May 1954 carried one other future General Authority who was going to visit a temple. The *Oronsay* stopped in Auckland, New Zealand, where a group of temple-bound Saints boarded. One of them was Douglas Martin, who was going to the Hawaiian Temple to be married to Wati Crawford. Douglas Martin would become a member of the First Quorum of the Seventy thirty-three years later, one year before Elder Sackley would be called to the same quorum.

In Cardston, Elder Sackley worked at odd jobs for a while and then was offered a job in Medicine Hat, 150 miles away, for a wholesale grocery company. He declined the position, telling the company president he had come halfway around the world to be near the temple, and Medicine Hat didn't qualify. Ironically, he spent the final years of his professional career in Medicine Hat, as vice president of administration and then as president of a government college there. By then, the Sackleys decided in family council, perhaps they could better serve the Lord doing missionary work in that remote community. In the interim he completed a bachelor's degree at Utah State University in Logan, Utah; received a certificate of municipal administration from the University of Alberta in Edmonton; and spent twenty-five years in education with the Cardston school district.

The family grew to love Canada as they became involved in the Church and community there, and the year they had planned to stay extended to thirty-five years. Their number increased by three sons, Ken, Peter, and Wayne Mark. Over the years Elder Sackley served as a stake missionary, elders quorum president, bishop, high councilor, stake clerk, and counselor in a stake presidency, while Sister Sackley's service included being president of the Primary and the Relief Society. But more important than the titles and positions to the Sackleys was the time they spent concentrating on "the one," extending eager, warm arms of fellowship and love to those around them, particularly those they felt were in need of the soothing balm of the gospel.

One such person was a fellow school administrator, also known as a prominent Mormon hater, who extended many invitations to Elder Sackley to go fishing with him. When at last Elder Sackley had an afternoon free, the two men went out in a boat together. There, as they sat placidly casting their lines into the lake and waiting for a bite, the man confided that he had once been a Latter-day Saint, but because he felt that other members had been unfair to him over the years, he had disassociated himself. Elder Sackley, he said, was the only Latter-day Saint he had any respect for or felt he could trust.

Distressed by these comments, Elder Sackley returned to his friend's home that evening. When the man found out Elder Sackley wanted to discuss the Church, he ordered him to leave.

"You opened the discussion yourself this afternoon," Elder Sackley told him, "and I'm not leaving until you hear me out. I love you," he continued. "I know without question that the Church is true and that you've made a shocking mistake with your own life. You've been driven out of the Church by your own foolishness and Word of Wisdom problems." The conversation continued, with neither man budging an inch. Finally, believing he had done all he could, yet reaffirming his faith in their friendship, Elder Sackley went home. Both were shaken and unsettled.

Several hours later, Elder Sackley was awakened by a telephone call from his friend. Through contrite tears, the man confessed he had been unable to sleep and asked Elder Sackley to please come back. They talked through the night, but this time the conversation was different, as the bitter, unrelenting shackles gradually began to soften and melt away from a long-troubled heart.

"As he struggled to return from thirty-five years of inactivity, he experienced some of the most terrible fear I've ever seen a man go through," Elder Sackley said. "He was afraid that if he went back to Church the building would fall on him or that people would smell the cigarette smoke on his clothes and mock or rebuff him. I told him I would handle anyone who did that." Together the two friends went to church. Not many months later his friend was sealed to his wife in the House of the Lord, and Elder Sackley was a witness.

An additional chapter of the story began twelve years later with another phone call. The Sackleys had since moved 450 miles away to Edmonton, and the call was from the man's wife, who told him her husband was dying of lung cancer, a victim of the cigarette habit he had kicked years ago. He had asked her to call his old friend. The next day Elder Sackley stood by the hospital bedside of his friend, who said, "I want to tell you something I've never told another man. I love you." He then requested that Elder Sackley speak at his funeral and "tell all of my rowdy friends to repent and change their lives." He had one more request: "I'm pretty sure you're going to make it to the celestial kingdom, but I'm not too certain about me. If I make it, will you look me up? I'd like to know we will meet on the other side."

Elder Sackley promised, and the men embraced. Three days later another call brought the news that his friend had died. "I loved that man," he says, then adds, with a twinkle in his eye, "We'll see each other again. We have an appointment to go home teaching together in heaven."

Part of Elder Sackley's effectiveness comes from the preciseness and promptness of his early home life, the self-control and discipline of an Australian commando, and genuine love for his fellowman. The remaining ingredient in his success comes from his devotion to the Lord and eagerness to obey without question. "I have only one reason for being a member of the Church. When I heard the gospel, it struck me like a thunderbolt. I am totally convinced of its truthfulness."

He was serving as college president in Medicine Hat when a call from President Spencer W. Kimball caused him once more to give up everything and move, this time to the Philippines as a mission president. The Sackleys sold their home and told their children to come with trucks and take whatever they wanted of their furnishings and belongings. Full-time Church service has become their way of life. Perhaps one day they will return to Edmonton, Alberta, but in the meantime, they have never looked back.

In 1979 Elder Sackley, accompanied by his wife, opened up the Philippines Quezon City Mission, and later he opened a mission in Baguio. In 1982 he was called to serve as administrative assistant and Sister Sackley was called as matron in the Salt Lake Temple. While in Salt Lake City, Elder Sackley was asked by the Canadian ministry of education to return to his career in education. "If we have anything left in life, we give it to The Church of Jesus Christ of Latter-day Saints, to which we owe our allegiance," he wrote in reply.

A year later Elder and Sister Sackley were called to direct the Washington Temple Visitors' Center, and in 1985 they were called to serve in the Sydney Australia Temple. "With that call they had come full circle," wrote a newspaper reporter. "They left their homeland in order to go to a temple; now they had returned to serve in a temple in their native country." (*Church News*, April 16, 1988, p. 10.)

In 1986 a new calling again changed their address, this time to the Nigeria Lagos Mission. Two years later Elder Sackley had just been directed to form the first black stake in the Church when a telephone call came from President Gordon B. Hinckley, and he was told that the Lord had called him to the First Quorum of the Seventy. (He became a member of the Second Quorum of the Seventy when it was organized in April 1989.) "I was nonplussed. Just a few weeks before I had received a letter from Salt Lake City asking me to spend an additional year in Nigeria, so this took me totally off guard." In Nigeria the missionaries had coped with the intense heat by wearing white shirts and ties but no suit coats.

He told President Hinckley, who asked him to return to Utah, "I will need to get some clothing. I don't have anything suitable." "Get some and come," was the reply.

Since becoming a Seventy, Elder Sackley has served as second counselor to the president of the British Isles/Ireland/ Africa Area, headquartered in Solihull, West Midlands, England. Although much of the time of a General Authority is taken up by administrative duties, Elder Sackley is determined not to lose one-on-one contact with the Saints. In every area they visit, he and Sister Sackley make special arrangements to visit those whom they feel they can serve in some way. Almost without exception they have been received with great joy into people's homes and hearts. "I've had a wandering life, but it's been a great life," Elder Sackley claims. "I've never regretted one minute. And it's been a great privilege to be married to a woman who feels exactly the same way."

The course of Elder Sackley's life was forever altered— and his feet forced onto the path that led to the gospel—by events put into motion after his near-fatal wounds in World War II. His favorite lines in Shakespeare come from the play *As You Like It:* "Sweet are the uses of adversity, / Which, like the toad, ugly and venomous, / Wears yet a precious jewel in his head." (Act II, sc. 1.) To this committed servant of the Lord, membership in the Church is a precious jewel indeed.

GERALD E. MELCHIN

Two downcast missionaries were trudging along a dusty street, a scene that has been duplicated time and again throughout the world; but this particular time was 1921 – ninety-one years after the restoration of the gospel – and the setting was the Eastern Canadian town of Kitchener, Ontario.

The pair were tired and discouraged, unable to find anyone interested in the message they had traveled half a continent to deliver. There had been little missionary activity in that part of Canada since John Taylor and his companions were there in the 1830s. If there were other Mormons in Kitchener, the missionaries didn't know who – or where – they were. Suddenly they heard the strains of a melody played on a phonograph, wafting out the open window of a nearby home. The song, a favorite LDS Church hymn, brightened

189

their spirits, and they proceeded up the sidewalk to the door to listen.

Amos Willis, noticing the two young men on his front porch, invited them in. A student of the Bible, he was immediately intrigued by their message of a "new" Christian religion. That meeting was the first of many others, and before long Amos embraced the gospel and was baptized a member of The Church of Jesus Christ of Latter-day Saints. The first of many Willis family members who eventually joined the Church through his influence, Amos became the nucleus of the Kitchener Branch, a tiny congregation that met in his living room — the same room where he was introduced to the gospel — for several years.

Rosetta, Amos's daughter, and her husband, Arthur Melchin, investigated the Church together. Although she was ready to be baptized, Arthur didn't feel that he had yet gained the testimony he was seeking; he also faced opposition from some members of his family. Then three-year-old Gerald, the younger of Arthur and Rosetta's two sons, became gravely ill with pneumonia. Everything medically possible was done to help him, but the doctors gave little hope, cautioning the young couple to prepare for their son's death.

Amos knew there was one more possibility to restore his grandson's health: he called in the elders to administer to the child. The effect was almost instantaneous. Gerald's rapid recovery was all that Arthur needed to complete his testimony; he had at last found an irrefutable reason to join the Church. Arthur and Rosetta were baptized May 11, 1923.

In the years following their baptism, the family accustomed themselves to living the gospel, becoming familiar with Church programs and activities. Gerald was born in Kitchener on May 14, 1921, and many of his earliest memories centered around Church meetings held in his grandfather's home with his parents, his older brother, Howard, and the handful of faithful Saints. Though many of his relatives on the Willis side joined the Church, his father was the only Melchin to do so. Mormons were few and far between in Kitchener — as they were in most of Eastern Canada — and Arthur and Rosetta longed to live and raise their sons in an atmosphere that was predominantly LDS. So in 1925, when Gerald was four and his brother, Howard, was ten, the family moved to Raymond, Alberta, leaving their kin far behind. Raymond was one of thirteen settlements in the southern part of the province colonized by the Latter-day Saints around the turn of the century. Through their move the Melchins were still about 750 miles north of Church headquarters in Salt Lake City, but they were surrounded by Mormon neighbors and felt themselves to be in the bosom of the Church.

Against that small-town backdrop, Gerald grew up secure and loved, becoming involved in the excellent provincial academic and athletic school programs. Though he enjoyed playing hockey and basketball, he couldn't be on the high school basketball team because of an after-school job. He earned a dollar a week as a janitor in the local movie theater, which was enough to buy his clothes and for spending money. (Coincidentally, the theater was owned by Lee Brewerton, father of Teddy E. Brewerton, who also became a member of the First Quorum of the Seventy. The boys, who were four years apart in age, grew up as friends, working together, later joining the air force at the same time, and eventually serving together as General Authorities.)

Rosetta Melchin was an affectionate, maternal woman who shared the hospitality of her home and table with neighbors, fellow Latter-day Saints, missionaries, and later, during World War II, men and women in military service. Gerald grew used to a home full of noisy, happy people, and he would often find ten or more at the dinner table, attracted

191

by the warm welcome and scrumptious breads, pies, and cookies from Rosetta's kitchen.

A gentle, quiet man, Arthur was a farmer at heart. Though he never had the money necessary for a farm of his own, he worked many years for the local agricultural college, raising prize-winning cattle. Later he worked for the sugar factory, Raymond's primary commercial enterprise.

Gerald's seventeenth year was a pivotal one in his life. His grandfather Melchin became very ill, and Arthur and Rosetta decided to move back to Kitchener in order to spend time with him before he died. Being uprooted in the middle of the school year from friends, school, and familiar surroundings was difficult for the teenager, who found little in common with the non-Mormon youths he encountered in Ontario. He and a cousin were the only teenagers in the Kitchener Branch, which by now had moved to a rented hall but was still only slightly larger than before. Though Gerald had never doubted the gospel teachings, this new situation forced him to solidify his testimony. He was often called on to speak or fulfill other assignments in the small branch, and he spent many hours working with the full-time missionaries. He also began to read the Book of Mormon, which became the foundation for his newfound strength.

Another advantage of the move was that Gerald became acquainted with many relatives who had previously been only names to him. He especially enjoyed talking about the gospel and other topics with his grandfather. Another influential adult from that year in Ontario was Eldon Willis, Gerald's uncle and the branch president. Eldon recognized the pitfalls inherent in the choices open to his nephew — either becoming involved with his peers, to whom drinking and smoking were an integral part of activities, or spending many hours alone. He and Gerald developed a close relationship, playing chess, going out for ice cream, or just talking together.

Gerald realized how much he had grown and changed when the family returned to Raymond the following year. The difference became clear one day when he was with some of his friends he had grown up with and the conversation turned to the Church. "I remember how shocked and disappointed I was when they said they didn't know if they believed the Joseph Smith story or if the Church was true," Elder Melchin reflected later. "I was shocked to hear them say that, because, like me, they had been in the Church all of their lives. It was really a sad experience for me."

A year after returning to Raymond, the Melchins moved again, this time to Winnipeg, Manitoba, where Arthur got a job at the sugar factory and Gerald enrolled in business college. While a student in 1942, he decided to serve a mission and was called to the Eastern Canadian Mission. Though he never returned to school (a fact he would view with some regret in later life), choosing a mission was an easy decision, for he had often heard his grandfather's conversion story and had also been able to serve with the missionaries in Kitchener, witnessing the blessings the gospel brings into the lives of converts.

For more than half of his mission Elder Melchin lived in the mission home in Toronto and served as mission secretary to three mission presidents. His second president, Joseph Quinney, died after suffering a heart attack one day while traveling by train to Montreal. While President Quinney was seventy-five years old at the time and had not been in good health, the missionaries were shocked by his passing. During the difficult days that followed, Elder Melchin served as temporary mission president, shouldering the responsibility for the missionaries in the field and the smooth running of the mission home. Because it was wartime and the few trains in operation were filled beyond capacity with troops, the new mission president, Octave Ursenbach, did not arrive for three months.

During that time Elder Melchin met a new missionary, Evelyn Knowles, from Ogden, Utah. She had been called to serve as a stenographer in the mission home, and right away Elder Melchin realized that she was different from any other woman he had ever known. She was beautiful, self-confident, spiritual, and talented, both as a singer and as a speaker — and, best of all, the attraction was mutual. With both of them assigned to the mission home, the two missionaries quickly became acquainted, though they were very careful to keep their relationship on an appropriate level.

By the conclusion of his mission a few months later, in 1944, Elder Melchin left Toronto knowing he had fallen in love, and he proposed to Evelyn by letter. While she may have been happy about the proposal, her parents back home were not so sure. When she wrote and told her family about it, her father hastily wrote back and said that he did not want his little girl marrying a stranger and moving "way up North."

At this juncture Sister Ursenbach, the mission mother, stepped in. She wrote to Evelyn's parents and lauded the character and accomplishments of Elder Melchin, concluding, "I would willingly line up my daughters, and Gerald Melchin could take his pick of them."

With this endorsement Evelyn's parents were mollified somewhat, though they were still unhappy about the prospect of their daughter and future grandchildren living so far away. But that was still in the future, for Evelyn's mission would last another year.

While he waited, Gerald joined the Royal Canadian Air Force and was sent to Edmonton, Alberta, for training as a wireless air gunner. The sudden transition from missionary to serviceman was a difficult one, offering a complete turnabout in life-styles, purposes, and environment. Commissioned as an officer just as the war was ending, he was one of the first servicemen released in April 1945, which also was the month Evelyn was released from her mission. On her way home to Utah, she stopped in Raymond to visit him. He was anxious for them to be together, so soon after her visit he followed her to Utah. On July 12, 1945, they were married in the Logan Temple.

The newlyweds made their home in Raymond and quickly became involved in Church, community, and business affairs. About a year after their marriage, they were visited in Raymond by Evelyn's parents. Though Gerald's new in-laws were initially unimpressed with the small town, which didn't even have a paved road, they were impressed by friendly, sincere townspeople and the warm reception they received—and they decided that maybe their daughter hadn't made such a bad match after all. Grandchildren started coming in 1947, when the Melchins' first son, Richard, was born; he was followed by Shauna, Gregory, Brook, Wade, and Barbara. Grandfather and Grandmother Knowles needn't have worried about their daughter's family living so far away from Ogden, for Gerald and Evelyn established a pattern of visiting in Utah several times a year, for holidays, birthdays, and other special occasions. "We wore out two cars traveling back and forth," he claims.

Gerald and Evelyn were called to serve as M-Men and Gleaner leaders in the Mutual Improvement Association. He was subsequently called as ward clerk and then as a seventy, while Evelyn began serving in the Primary. She also took piano lessons and joined community and Church choirs. Before her mission she had taken vocal lessons, and her teacher had told her she had a great deal of potential and that to abandon her study for religious service was folly. Although Evelyn never did sing professionally, music has always been a large part of her life, and she feels that her life and the lives of her family have been enriched by it. She has never regretted her choice.

Gerald and Howard had long wanted to go into business together, so when Gerald returned to Raymond after his military service, he and his brother, Howard, formed an automobile dealership. In 1949, on a trip to Toronto to buy cars for their dealership, Gerald saw some auto transports and wondered if there might possibly be a future in that business. When he returned home, he shared his feelings with Howard, and they decided to expand their operations. They bought some auto transports, hired drivers, and were soon in an additional business. They had tough competition from the railroads, which were supported by government subsidies and could afford to undercut competitors, and several times it looked as if the business would go under. At the point of greatest financial difficulty, when they were faced with having to expand the size of their trailers to conform to new government regulations, both their banker and their finance company advised them to quit and declare bankruptcy.

Uncertain what to do, the brothers went for advice to a long-time friend, a patriarch in the Church. The three knelt in prayer, and he blessed the brothers that they would have peace of mind. "I promise you that if you pay your tithes and serve the Lord, you will prosper," he said, adding, "It may take time, but don't quit. You will be able to carry on with your business and support your families despite the problems." At that time, Gerald recommitted himself to do whatever the Lord asked him to do. With the peace of mind that followed the blessing, he said, "I was able to devote my evenings to family and the Church without worrying about the business."

Soon afterwards they sat down with their banker and figured out a refinancing plan. Some time later, while Howard was in Windsor, Ontario, a representative of a large auto company called and offered him and Gerald a big increase in business if they would agree to put all of their transport equipment at his exclusive disposal. It sounded too good to be true, and as the brothers talked about it over the phone, they felt they would be foolish not to seize the opportunity. But after they hung up, Gerald received a prompting that they should not become involved with this deal. He called Howard back and explained what had happened, and as a result, they turned the deal down. The auto company quit doing business with them, but eventually those dealers who had received similar offers and stayed with it were forced out of business as the company reneged on its promises. Gerald and Howard's business, however, soon became a major transporter for General Motors. It took about ten years before all of the financial problems were ironed out, but eventually they were able to repay all of their creditors. By 1959 the business had grown so large that it was no longer feasible to remain in Raymond, and they moved to Calgary. They sold the auto dealership and continued to expand the transport business, and eventually it became the largest company of its kind in Western Canada.

Not long after their move to Calgary, an opportunity to keep his commitment to do anything the Lord asked came to Gerald from an unexpected direction. He and Evelyn were called to be the stake dance directors.

"He'll never do that," Evelyn said, laughing, when she heard about the position.

Gerald felt that he had two left feet, and he did not relish the idea of teaching something he knew very little about. He told the stake president he would be happy to accept any other assignment, and the president responded, "We sure wish you'd do it anyway." To Evelyn's surprise, her husband accepted the challenge—with reservations, but without further hesitation. Afterward, the stake president, N. Eldon Tan-

197

ner, remarked that he knew just what kind of man Brother Melchin was when he accepted that calling.

"After the commitment I had made to the Lord, there was nothing I could do but say 'I will,'" Elder Melchin recalls. He and Evelyn attended a training session in Lethbridge, where they were lost in the swirl of seemingly experienced dancers. "We were the only ones on the floor who didn't seem to know the steps or the terms," he says, a twinkle in his eyes, as he clearly savors the memory. "I could read the steps and my wife had the rhythm, so we went home and together studied the books and taught ourselves the dances while our children looked on." They put on a successful dance festival that year and another one twelve months later. And, to his surprise, Gerald felt a twinge of disappointment when he was released as dance director soon after this and called to serve in the Young Men's Mutual Improvement Association presidency. He and Evelyn continued to enjoy dancing together for several years.

Not long after the Melchins moved to Calgary, their seventh child, Barbara, was born with a serious congenital heart problem. The valves and chambers of her heart had not developed properly, and, weak and pale, she failed to thrive. At six months of age, she had a heart attack and went into heart failure. Her parents rushed her to the hospital, where the doctors gave her little hope of survival. Laying their hands on her tiny head, Gerald and their bishop gave the tiny girl a priesthood blessing. "I knew instantly that she would be all right," he says. Though they were in for a long and difficult struggle, Barbara did pull through, and today she is a grown woman, married and raising a family.

"I have received so many blessings and witnessed so many miracles, that I have a very real testimony about the power of the priesthood," says Elder Melchin, recalling the blessing that saved his own life at age two. "That's one advantage to being called to leadership positions — it gives more opportunities to use your priesthood. I've had many chances to give blessings to my family and see those blessings become a reality." One such opportunity came when he gave a father's blessing to one of his sons who was leaving on a mission. "I told him he would baptize many people, and I felt foolish the minute I said it, because France is a very difficult mission field, and if you can baptize one person . . . " He pauses, at a loss for words, then adds with a sense of wonder, "he had thirty-two baptisms."

Three years after moving to Calgary, Gerald was called to be bishop of the Calgary Third Ward, and four years after that, president of the newly created Calgary North Stake. Evelyn served in the Young Women's program and as ward and then stake Relief Society president, and she also shared her musical talents by singing solos and directing choirs.

In 1972, after serving as stake president for six years, Elder Melchin was called to preside over the California Arcadia Mission. With no regrets, the Melchin brothers sold their auto transport business. Then, with the two oldest children married and the next two in college, Gerald and Evelyn, accompanied by their three youngest children and a foster daughter from the Indian Placement Program, moved to California.

Elder Melchin thoroughly enjoyed his new assignment, calling it the "best job in the Church, next to being a bishop." He enjoyed full-time Church service as well as working with young people. Because the mission boundaries were small enough for him to travel anywhere in the mission and still be at home that night, he held many district meetings and conferences, training the missionaries and getting to know each personally, and Sister Melchin organized choirs among the enthusiastic missionaries and members. Morale was high and the mission was blessed with much success.

Returning to Calgary in 1975, Gerald and Evelyn — their

business sold and children raised—found they had an ample supply of something they'd never experienced before: time. Before their mission they had always been busy, many of their activities pressed on them by the necessities of home, family, Church, and business. Now they had the luxury of increased control over their time and resources and making conscious choices about the substance of their lives. Gerald began working with a son and a son-in-law in their respective business ventures. They visited with their children and grand-children and were able to travel to the United States to visit relatives and abroad to France and Israel. Gerald served in the Church as a stake high councilor, as a gospel doctrine teacher, and eventually as the Calgary welfare region agent, charged with the assignment of overseeing construction of a new welfare cannery.

Yet, as much as they enjoyed each aspect of their lives, Gerald had a vague feeling of unfulfillment, a sense that something was missing. One day in 1984, while climbing the hills above Logan, Utah, where they were visiting, he pondered his life and his service to the Lord. "I told the Lord that I wasn't satisfied with the way I was using all of my time, that I felt I had more time and effort that could be used in his service," he recalls. "I was ready for whatever he wanted me to do, wherever he wanted me to go."

When he returned to his hotel room, the phone was ringing. It was Elder Loren C. Dunn of the First Quorum of the Seventy, who wanted to meet with him. The result was a call to serve as a regional representative, a position he held for four years, presiding over regions in Calgary, Edmonton, and Southern Alberta.

One afternoon in late September 1988, Elder and Sister Melchin were traveling to Salt Lake City to attend general conference and the regional representatives' seminar when another significant phone call came. President Thomas S.

Monson's secretary was calling to arrange a meeting between President Monson and Elder and Sister Melchin on Friday morning.

When the three met at the scheduled time, President Monson asked the Melchins about their health and if they loved one another. When those answers were affirmative, he dropped the bombshell: Would Elder Melchin accept a call to became a General Authority, a member of the Second Quorum of the Seventy?

"It is a question that upsets everything," says Elder Melchin, "all of your plans and ideas about your future, your equilibrium, your stomach. I felt as if I had been blown into a state of confusion." He accepted the calling and, for the second time in his life, began severing ties and obligations in Calgary in order to go where the Lord wanted him to serve, this time in Salt Lake City.

His first assignments were in the presidency of the Utah North Area and on the general temple committee. In October 1989, his assignments were changed to the Utah South Area and the committee for the restoration of blessings. It is the latter responsibility that Elder Melchin finds particularly poignant, as he and two other General Authorities review applications from members who have been excommunicated or those seeking cancellations of sealings.

"It is an assignment that requires you to rely heavily on the Spirit of the Lord as you make recommendations to the First Presidency that vitally affect people's lives," he explains. "It can be very difficult, but also extremely rewarding. Each case is a lesson of hardship, heartache, and disappointment."

Those close to Gerald Melchin know him as a man of deep, tender feelings. As he talks about his life, whether it be Church assignments, family, or his blessings and trials, his emotions are often close to the surface. One experience particularly close to his heart involved his youngest child,

Barbara, and her husband, who, at the time Elder Melchin was called as a General Authority, had recently learned they were expecting a baby. Because of her heart condition, Barbara had had to be especially careful all her life to avoid strenuous activity. Now a team of medical specialists warned her that a pregnancy would probably be fatal, both to herself and to the child she was carrying; her heart was barely strong enough to sustain her, let alone another. But with the united faith and prayers of the family, including a priesthood blessing from her father, the couple felt strongly about going through with the pregnancy. They had received the witness they needed that abortion was not the answer, and that this special child needed only to receive a mortal body. Barbara's faith and courage sustained her in making the critical decision and through the difficult weeks as the pregnancy progressed.

The doctors had hoped the baby would make it through gestation as far as twenty-five weeks, but by twenty weeks it wasn't getting enough nourishment. A Cesarian section was performed. The tiny, perfectly developed boy, born much too soon and weighing just a pound, lived only four days. Though the experience was traumatic for the anguished parents, their grief was assuaged by the knowledge that they had done the right thing and that their infant son was in the hands of the Lord. Barbara slowly regained her health, and the couple were later able to adopt a baby girl.

"When I gave Barbara the blessing, I had such a strong impression that she would live that I didn't doubt it for a moment, though I didn't know what would happen to the baby. The whole thing was a very difficult experience. But when the child passed away in his parents' arms, there was such a strong spirit present that overall it was very comforting and healing. It has been a special experience for our family."

Family has always been the top priority for Gerald and Evelyn Melchin. Theirs is large and close-knit family, accustomed to spending a lot of time together, whether gathering on Sunday evening at Grandma and Grandpa's, or spending time every summer at the family's cabin at a mountain lake. In fact, the most difficult change in their lives as a result of Elder Melchin's calling as a General Authority has been their move from Calgary, where most of their children have settled, and the separation from their grandchildren, missing the stages of their growth and development, and the celebrations and crises of their young lives.

Yet, despite their wish to be reunited with their progeny, the Melchins' desire to serve in any way the Lord requires is stronger. They do not plan to rush back to Canada when he is released; they may linger in Salt Lake City to do genealogy and temple work. The peace of mind that comes from being focused single-mindedly on the Lord's work has proved invigorating. At an age when most couples are nestled comfortably into retirement, Gerald and Evelyn Melchin are enjoying their second wind, working harder than ever, with eternal perspectives and goals.

CARLOS H. AMADO

The man at the pulpit spoke simply, yet with great emotion. His words were seasoned by his mother tongue, and at times he struggled with semantics and pronunciation. Yet, instead of creating a barrier between himself and his listeners, his rich Spanish accent seemed only to intensify the message. As the audience listened in rapt attention, it was as though the essence of his soul poured out in his words.

He told of an anguished friend whose teenage son had died tragically in an accident; of the heartache borne by a childless couple struggling to come to terms with repeated miscarriages; of the death of his own father, leaving his mother widowed with fifteen children.

"Those who have gone through this kind of trial recognize that there are tragedies that are so difficult we cannot understand them," he said. "When trials come, it is time to turn our souls to God, who is the author of life and the only source of comfort." (*Ensign*, November 1989, p. 29.)

With these words, the general membership of the Church became acquainted with Elder Carlos H. Amado, who was speaking in general conference for the first time since being sustained as a member of the Second Quorum of the Seventy six months earlier, in April 1989. They discovered what the Saints in Guatemala have known and loved for many years, that Elder Amado—whose name means "beloved" in Spanish—is a leader with compassion, humility, and unquestioning devotion to the Lord.

"Those who suffer great adversity and sorrow and go on to serve their fellowmen develop a great capacity to understand others," he continued in his address. "Like the prophets, they have acquired a higher understanding of the mind and will of Christ. . . . The greatest tragedy that can happen to a person is not the loss of his possessions, or his intellect, or his mortal life, but rather to lose eternal life, which is the free gift of God." (Ibid.)

This testimony has become an absolute part of Elder Amado's existence. Because of the political, economic, and social instability in some Central American countries, he has encountered potentially perilous circumstances through his service to the Lord. While serving as a mission president in Guatemala and El Salvador, he and his missionaries occasionally found themselves "in jeopardy, where we needed to be alert and very cautious." Though they were often confronted with violence and upheaval caused by attacks of guerrilla forces and other troublesome factions, "the Lord always kept us out of danger and inspired us to do the right things. Because of his guidance and protection, we could do our work without concern about the things that were happening around us."

Elder Amado derives great comfort and courage from his

205

faith, which sustains him through difficult situations. He is hesitant to speak of specific incidents in which his life and the lives of others were preserved because of the sacred, personal nature of such experiences and because he is afraid others will view the events as "isolated miracles," when they are, in truth, part of the larger overall plan of the Lord.

"The promises the Lord has given to those who lose their lives while in his service are beautiful," he explains. "Only the Lord knows when I will die, but if I do, it will not happen before I can deliver the message the Lord wants his children to hear. After that it doesn't matter what happens to me." Elder Amado admits that although the Lord protects his servants, occasionally it becomes necessary for them to die as a testimony against iniquity, as in the case of the wicked King Noah and the prophet Abinadi. (See Mosiah 17.) Speaking of those killed in the Lord's service, he comments, "My concern is not for those who die, but for those who kill the Lord's messengers. They are the ones in a bad situation."

Another reason Elder Amado prefers not to dwell on the dangers he has encountered is that he does not see them as impediments to his service. Rather, the emphasis of his labors in the Lord's vineyards is love, and his message is one of joy, hope, and eternal peace. It is a message that the people of Guatemala and of other Latin American countries are receiving hungrily, resulting in explosive growth of the Church in those areas.

The conversion of Elder Amado and his family in 1956, and his subsequent development in spirituality and leadership to the point where he was sustained as a General Authority nearly thirty-four years later, parallels the growth and maturity of the Church in Guatemala. When he was baptized, he became a member of the Guatemala City Branch, the only branch in the large capital city. The three and a half decades have been fruitful for the Amado family and for many others like them; Guatemala by 1990 had seventeen stakes—eleven in Guatemala City alone—with more than 57,000 members.

Elder Amado's call as a Seventy was greeted with joy and enthusiasm by his fellow Guatemalans, who were pleased at the calling of a known, beloved leader, but also at the symbolic coming of age of the Church in Guatemala, signified by having their "own" General Authority. At forty-four years of age— the youngest General Authority at the time of his call—Elder Amado is representational of the Church in his homeland, full of the vigor and strength of youth, yet surprisingly wise and mature for his years. He stands five feet seven inches and has a medium frame and black hair, and what one first notices is the twinkle in his black eyes and the boyish grin that spreads from ear to ear. He and his wife, the former Mayavel Piñeda, are the parents of five.

Elder Amado was born in Guatemala City September 25, 1944, the third of fifteen children born to Carlos and Rosario Albertina Funes Amado. His father was an auto mechanic who usually held down two or three jobs in order to support his large family. Money was one of the few things in short supply in the Amado household, where there was an abundance of people, animals, chores, diapers, laundry, and fun.

But there can be many positives about having the house always full of people, including members of the immediate family, neighbors, relatives, and friends. "With so many brothers and sisters, it was practically impossible to say about anything, 'This is exclusively mine,' and so we learned to share everything," Elder Amado explains. "My parents were happy people who loved children. I remember that Mother— who always seemed to be expecting, with another baby nestled in her arms and several small children clustered around her—was constantly singing. Father, whenever he was home, was invariably helping another child or two, or holding them on his lap."

With a house continuously burgeoning with children—
even if each one only invited a single friend over, the numbers
were daunting—there was plenty of noise and activity. One
particular morning, when there was a typical crowd around
and Albertina had gone to the market, a pillow fight broke
out. By the time she returned home, her son remembers,
"everything was dirty, everyone was unclean. Oh, my poor
mother," he laments. "She needed to wash again all of the
clothes, and all by hand—we had no washing machine. Of
course we helped her." He pauses, shaking his head at the
memory, then adds with characteristic understatement, "but
having so many children was a tremendous challenge."

The boisterous, fun-loving family learned to work hard
together and also to play together. "We didn't have much,
but we learned to make do with very little. There were always
plenty of people around to play with," Elder Amado explains.
"I loved sports, and if I had a ball, that was enough for me.
I might have no food, no clothes, no anything; but if I had
a ball, I was happy." Although it was difficult to find the time
or space for occasional privacy, Carlos enjoyed his seven
brothers and seven sisters and grew up with a sense of pro-
tectiveness toward them.

Besides sports, the Amado children enjoyed going to the
movies—"and I still do, although it's hard to find any good
ones to go to today," Elder Amado interjects. Sunday seemed
to be the best day to go, and Albertina had no objections to
that, so long as her children attended mass in their Catholic
parish first. "So sometimes we children went to church because it was a requirement to do the things we wanted to
do," he explains, but that was the extent of religious influence
in his early childhood.

With no automobile and no money to take a bus, the
Amados also spent a lot of time walking together to and from
school, various other activities, and, after they joined the

Church, the branch chapel, which was about three miles from their home. They were happy walks, with plenty of time for conversation, singing, games, and good-natured competitions. "Whenever we went to school or to an activity, if there were not many others there, we were enough. If I went to a party, I could always dance with two or three of my sisters. It didn't matter who else showed up, we always had a good time with ourselves."

Carlos was nine years old when two North American missionaries came to their home. His father, eager to practice his English, invited the young men in. It wasn't long before his interest in the missionaries focused on their message and not their language, however, for he had been searching for the true religion for many years.

Young Carlos attended his first LDS meeting with suspicion; he had heard of other religious groups that had boisterous services with loud singing and wild gesturing, and he wanted no part of it. But after being in the meetinghouse for only a few minutes, he learned two things: the atmosphere was different than he had feared it might be and, more importantly, the Church sponsored the Scouting program. His reservations vanished and he began to embrace this new religion enthusiastically. For the next two years the Amados continued to learn about the Church and incorporated every aspect of the gospel into their lives.

"At that time you had to fulfill a lot of requirements to join the Church," says Elder Amado. "The gospel was new and strange in Guatemala, and the missionaries wanted to be sure investigators fully understood and had a testimony of the doctrines before they were baptized. So for two years they tested us. My father was impatient to join the Church; he was doing everything he could do—fasting, praying, studying, paying tithing, and serving as the young men's president—and he didn't like waiting." Finally, Carlos and

Albertina Amado and their six oldest children were baptized in 1956, with the distinction of being the largest family ever to join the Church in Guatemala. The five younger children, along with the four more who were born later, were baptized as they came of age.

"When I was a young child, I discovered how many we were and that my parents did not have enough to cover our necessities. I used to wonder why, if we did not have enough to go around, my parents kept having more children," Elder Amado admits. "But when I joined the Church, I began to recognize that it was not an accident that I was born in my family, and that each one of my brothers and sisters was a blessing in my life. Once I began to understand that having children is a privilege and a blessing, I began to better appreciate them.

"I remember the day the doctor talked to my parents and said it was not possible for my mother to have any more children. Both of my parents cried a lot and I didn't understand why. After all, they already had fifteen children. But my father told me, 'One day you will understand how much your mother and I love each other and how much we love children.' They really did love us," he adds reflectively. And the Amado children loved each other. Even though today they are scattered throughout North and Central America, they still have a warm relationship and enjoy being together and rekindling childhood memories.

When Carlos was fourteen, a desire to fulfill a mission was planted in his heart, and it continued to grow as he grew. He finished secondary school and then obtained a degree in drafting from the Technical Vocational Institute of Guatemala City. At seventeen he discussed his goal with the mission president, who told him that to go on a mission, he would need to pay half of the amount himself, a sum of almost twenty-five hundred dollars, and then the mission president would help him find a source for the other half. Since most of his meager earnings as a draftsman went to his father to help support his younger brothers and sisters, the amount needed for a mission seemed out of reach. But his mother encouraged him to strive for his goal, insisting to her husband, "We must never deny him the privilege to serve the Lord."

It took Carlos four years to accumulate the money for a mission, four long, often disappointing years in which he paid his tithing, gave half of the remainder to his parents, and saved what was left. "My parents didn't require me to do that, but I could see that at the end of the month often many things were still needed, and I wanted to do my part. But I had a hard time understanding why the mission president told me what he did. I had a very good friend who only had to contribute ten dollars a month for his mission, and his parents paid that!"

It was difficult for Carlos to sit through his friends' mission farewells, have them serve two years, and then attend their homecomings, while he was still waiting to go. "They would come home so enthused, telling me how happy they were serving as missionaries, and then ask me that cruel question, 'When are you going on your mission?'"

One such person was his older sister's boyfriend, whom Carlos taught the gospel, emphasizing the importance of missionary service, and then baptized. When the young man then went on a mission, Carlos was even more confused and unhappy. "I was crying inside," he says. "I couldn't understand why, if I had a righteous desire, it was so difficult to achieve. I had so much opposition." But still he did not waver in his desire to be a missionary or in his faith in the gospel and his leaders, including the mission president.

"Though I didn't understand at the time, I am grateful to him now because I learned some valuable lessons," says Elder Amado. "The experience taught me the importance of

211

working hard to fulfill a goal. I also learned that the more you sacrifice for something, the more you appreciate it once it becomes yours, and the more seriously you take your assignment."

Finally, when he was twenty-two years old, Carlos had accumulated the required amount. A missionary couple from the United States who learned of his story told him that when they got home, they would finance the remaining 50 percent of his mission expenses. The papers were finally sent to Salt Lake City—and twice they were lost in the mail and had to be resubmitted. "The more I desired to go on a mission, the more challenges I had," recalls Elder Amado. "But now I realize that opposition is a part of happiness, and the more that you try to do a good thing, the more difficult it is. Today when I discover all of the challenges the members in our area face, the more convinced I am that we are doing the right thing!"

Carlos finally received his mission call, to the Andes Peru Mission. He would be the first native Guatemalan to serve a mission outside Central America. After two fruitful years, he wasn't ready to be released and asked his mission president to grant him a six-month extension. The president instead gave him only two weeks more, telling the eager missionary it was time he went home and faced other challenges, including education and marriage. Four others in the Amado family, including his mother, eventually also served missions.

Shortly after he returned home, his family moved to California and asked him to go with them. His older sister had previously gotten a job in San Francisco and made arrangements for the rest of the family to follow. But Carlos felt there was a divine purpose in his being born in Guatemala and that the Lord wanted him to stay and work there. He began studying architecture at the University of San Carlos in Guatemala City, while at the same time working as a draftsman and serving concurrently as the stake mission president, Sunday School president, and priests advisor. About this time he was also the chorister for the ward choir, and one of the choir members was a pretty, seventeen-year-old girl, Mayavel Piñeda. Her family had joined the Church when Mayavel was four, and she and Carlos had known each other as children. Then the Piñedas lived in El Salvador for five years, so he had not seen her for some time. Now the two had many choice opportunities to become acquainted with each other and with one another's dreams and goals as he walked her home from choir practices. Later they found out that they had each been impressed with the same things.

"I discovered that she had a strong testimony of the gospel and wanted to marry a returned missionary in the temple," says Elder Amado. "When I learned of this I fell in love with her, because I was watching for a very spiritual woman. Of course, she is also very beautiful — an extra blessing," he adds.

Mayavel was undoubtedly attracted to him and impressed when she found out he was a returned missionary. But despite her tender years, she was very serious-minded and sure of what she wanted. She was also very cautious. When he proposed a year later, she explains, "I knew I had feelings for him, but I didn't want to make a mistake." She fasted and prayed and asked herself, "What kind of father am I planning to give my children? Is my home going to enjoy all of the blessings of the priesthood? Is he the kind of person who will take me to the temple and lead my family into eternal life?" As she pondered these questions, she knew Carlos Amado was the right man for her. They were married in December 1971. Later they were sealed in the Oakland Temple, where they traveled so his family could attend the ceremony.

Their first child, Carlos Josue, was born in 1973, and another son, David, was born eleven months later. Carlos worked as a draftsman for two different companies and also began his own business, and with so many involvements, he did not complete his architectural degree, which he regrets. "In order to support my growing family, I became interested in earning money," he says. "Additionally, I was having a lot of success in my career and so I didn't pay enough attention to school."

Carlos did devote attention to the Church. Over the years he served as branch president, bishop, counselor in a stake presidency, stake president, and regional representative. In 1973, he began teaching seminary, a new program in Guatemala. It was a calling he loved. "Teaching seminary is the best way to keep in touch with the youth," he explains. Two years later he was hired to work in the Church Educational System, and within three months he became area director in Guatemala, a position he held for fourteen years, until he was called to the Second Quorum of the Seventy. He never regretted giving up his career as a draftsman.

Busy years have followed close after one another for the Amados, who added three more children to their family: Juan Pablo, who was born in 1978; Andres, 1979; and Mayavel, their only daughter, 1981. They have also been busy years for the Church in Guatemala, which has mushroomed in size. "The people in Latin America are very receptive to the gospel because their cultures are built on loyalty and commitment, as well as traditional family-centered values," Elder Amado explains. "So when we hear about the teachings of the Church, they seem natural to us, easy for us to believe in."

In 1980 Elder Amado was called to be president of the Guatemala City Mission, one of the two missions in the country. One day toward the end of his missionary assignment, which generally lasts three years, he and Sister Amado had to go to Mexico City on Church business. Unable to get a direct flight, they made reservations for a flight that made a stop in El Salvador, which borders on Guatemala. As they flew over that troubled country, both had strong feelings that it was time to reopen the El Salvador Mission, which had been closed for about three years because of political instability. Similar feelings on the way home caused them to begin to talk, fast, and pray about the matter. In the summer of 1982, Elder Amado was asked to reopen missionary work in El Salvador and to serve as president there, in addition to presiding over his current mission. With the help of ten elders, Salvadorans who were serving in the Guatemala City Mission, he reopened the mission, to the delight of the 25,000 or so Latter-day Saints there.

"I will always remember the feelings of the members and missionaries in El Salvador and the way the Lord protected us," he recalls. "It didn't matter how much conflict there was in that country, the spirit of the Lord guided us to avoid problems with the government, guerrillas, bombs, and everything. The Lord kept us out of danger." He served as mission president in El Salvador for one year, and a total of four years in Guatemala.

Shortly after being released from his mission in 1984, Elder Amado became chairman of the Guatemala City Temple committee, just five months before the temple was to be dedicated. He and the members in Guatemala "saw miracles happen" as they struggled with a rigorous completion schedule, attended to last-minute details, and strived to get the temple prepared for the dedication.

"Being the chairman of that committee was one of the best experiences of my life," Elder Amado says. "We felt the Lord's love for us as we completed that work. We also discovered that if we did everything we could do, the Lord would make up the difference." In the last hectic weeks before the dedication, "we often worked from five A.M. until two the next morning, organizing and even helping with the interior finishing work ourselves."

215

They felt it was all worth it when the temple was completed on schedule and they saw how impressed many of their countrymen were at the open house held prior to the dedication. "When the temple was dedicated, immediately we knew that the Lord had accepted it," he adds.

The members have received many blessings as a result of having a temple in their midst, Elder Amado reports. It has served as a focal point for members' commitment and dedication, as well as helping them to better understand their relationship to God. Great sacrifice is required of many of those who work in the temple and those who frequently attend sessions there, because of the extremely humble circumstances in which they live, the costs of transportation to the temple, the need to take time from their jobs and families, and other costs associated with temple attendance. "But the Lord blesses them and they discover it is not a sacrifice," he explains. "Although they do not receive an increase in their salaries, they find at the end of the month that they have enough to meet their basic needs, whereas those who are working for the same amount but not attending the temple often find themselves suffering at the end of the month with not enough for food and clothing.

"We traditionally believe that if we sacrifice to serve the Lord, that we will be blessed with more money. But usually that is not the case. We may receive monetary blessings, in that we spend what we have more wisely or we find our resources go further. For example, those who pay their tithing find they can live at the same level — or on an even higher level — as those who make the same amount but don't pay a percentage to the Lord. He also blesses us with spiritual blessings, increased understanding, and eternal priorities."

Elder Amado cites the example of two of his acquaintances. In the 1970s one, a well-to-do lawyer with a large, expensively furnished home, was not a member of the

216

Church. The second, who was also affluent, was a Latter-day Saint and gave much of his time and resources in service to the Lord. When Guatemala was hit by a destructive earthquake in 1976, the homes of both men were destroyed. "The lawyer came to me in tears, saying, 'I have lost my home, I have lost everything I had,' " recalls Elder Amado. "But the other man viewed things differently. 'I have been blessed. I only lost my house,' he said. Although they both lost the same amount materially, one had so much left, while the other had nothing."

In March 1989, Elder Amado, who was serving as a regional representative for the second time, received a call from the First Presidency's office asking him and Sister Amado to attend general conference in April. A few days later, President Thomas S. Monson, second counselor in the First Presidency, told Elder Amado he was being called to the Second Quorum of the Seventy. "I was holding the hand of my wife. I just squeezed her hand so tight and both of us closed our eyes and began to cry. Neither of us believed this could happen to us. When they had asked that my wife come with me, I knew something was going to happen. Perhaps I would be asked to serve again as a mission president, but I never, *never* imagined I would be called as a General Authority."

There are times when it is still difficult for him to believe. Ever since he first heard of the Church, Elder Amado had looked to the General Authorities as role models and had tried to learn everything he could about them and to pattern his life after theirs. "I would read and study about them, respect and admire them, but I never believed I would sit down among them," he says. "Among the General Authorities I am the youngest in age, and I also feel like I am the youngest in every way—learning, experience, knowledge. I am very happy to be closer to them, because it is a great opportunity to learn more about the Lord's servants. I still look to them as a great example for me."

Elder Amado recognizes that now, perhaps, others will be looking up to him in much the same way. "I weigh my words and actions carefully, because many members expect me to do everything right. But I am human and I make mistakes, which is not a problem for me, because if I make a mistake I can repent and be forgiven. But if the Church or any member were to be hurt because of something that I did . . . " He pauses, searching for the right words to express his feelings, then adds, "I love Christ with all of my heart and I love the prophet with all of my heart. It is a heavy responsibility to teach the same principles they are teaching." The challenges are actually increased, he believes, for both him and Elder Horacio Tenorio, who was called as a Seventy at the same time, for they are both Lamanites and are serving as role models to the great numbers of Lamanite members and converts.

Elder Amado's first assignment as a Seventy was to serve as second counselor in the Mexico/Central America Area, with headquarters in Mexico. He and Sister Amado have always sustained and supported each other in their responsibilities, considering that an important part of their duties as husband and wife and as parents. Their children also take the responsibilities of their parents' callings seriously, feeling the need to be examples of the Lord's teachings. The family enjoys participating in sports together — table tennis, soccer, and basketball — and camping and visiting interesting historical sites. Elder Amado enjoys running, arising at five o'clock several mornings a week to run three to five miles. Sister Amado, a good cook, enjoys preparing different kinds of cuisine for her family. "If we go to a restaurant and eat something we like, a week later she will have figured out how to make it and will fix the same dish even better for us," says Elder Amado.

The main element that has always drawn the couple — and now their children — together is their love for the Lord and their desire to do his will. When Elder Amado was released as mission president, he served for a time as Blazer leader, teaching ten- and eleven-year-old boys in Primary. "He prepared with as much thoroughness and love for his Primary lesson as he would for a presentation to a group of priesthood leaders," Sister Amado reports.

It is a commitment typical of the Amados, who belong to the first generation of members in Guatemala who have grown up in the Church. Elder Amado's decision to remain in Guatemala and not move to the United States with his parents has proven fruitful, not only for himself and his family, but also for many of his fellow Latter-day Saints in Mexico and Central America. "We have come a long way from the time when there was only a single branch in all of Guatemala," he reminisces. "Yet as rapidly as the Lamanites have accepted the gospel in the past, the rate of conversions will only increase in the years to come, because about 65 percent of all Guatemalans are of pure Lamanite descent. These are the children of the promise, and those promises are being fulfilled."

If they are, it is due in large part to faithful servants like Carlos H. Amado.

HORACIO A. TENORIO

Early in 1969, Horacio Tenorio was a sales manager and purchasing agent for a major telephone cable manufacturing company in Mexico City, Mexico. As a university graduate‑ with a degree in business, Horacio was a valued employee with a bright future. His job entailed many public relations duties, including entertaining clients, often in the more glamorous establishments in the city.

But more important to him than his career or business contacts was his family — his wife and three little girls — whom Horacio loved deeply and whose happiness and well-being he was eager to safeguard. Through his job, he was often aware of many undesirable elements of society, and he and his wife, Teresa, were becoming increasingly uneasy about the unsettled conditions of the world around them. They felt that crime, immorality, and disrespect for law and authority had combined to create an undesirable place for raising their daughters—Maria Teresa, ten; Monica, seven; and Rocio, five. Believing that perhaps the problem was the burgeoning metropolis, they considered moving to another locale with improved conditions. But after investigating other options—elsewhere in the country as well as in the world—they concluded that the situation was much the same everywhere.

"What will happen to my daughters as they grow up and go out into the world? Just what kind of a world are we living in? What is there to count on, to believe in? How can I prepare them to lead happy, fulfilled lives?" These and other questions tortured the thirty-three-year-old father as he searched for answers. His anxiety deepened until he found himself unable to sleep, spending long nights tossing and turning, filled with worry.

Finally, in despair Horacio turned to God. Never before had he considered himself a religious man; he called himself Catholic, but Catholicism had never played a role in his life beyond the few ceremonial functions he had attended in his early youth. Now fear and consternation directed his thoughts heavenward in a desperate, last-ditch plea. "Father, help me find a way to keep my family safe and clean," he prayed.

Within a few weeks the answer to his prayer entered his life, though it would be months before he would recognize it as the solution he was seeking. It came simply, unobtrusively one evening when his wife mentioned a conversation she had had that day with two young Americans who called themselves Mormons.

Actually the wheels had been set in motion about two weeks earlier when Teresa was visiting with her mother, who lived a few kilometers away. While she was there, two Mormon missionaries had knocked at the door. "Tell them I am not at home and send them away," her mother said, refusing to come out. Now the young men had returned when Teresa

221

was again at her mother's home. Embarrassed to tell them a second time that her mother wasn't there, she invited them in and began talking to them. Her mother stayed in the back room while Teresa and her thirteen-year-old sister received the first discussion.

Though Horacio could sense her excitement, he replied pessimistically, "Oh, the Mormons. They are the people that have many wives."

"No, no, that is not true," she responded, handing him some pamphlets they had given her. "Why don't you read these and then tell me what is wrong with what they say?" After reading the materials, though he knew little about religious matters, Horacio was certain they were not true.

"I have another appointment with them tomorrow evening," she said, adding a subtle challenge, "Why don't you come with me, and you can tell them that yourself?"

Thus began the first in a continual chain of meetings. Every evening for the next three months Horacio and Teresa met with the missionaries. Their own home, they found out later, was outside the missionaries' district, so they continued to meet at Teresa's mother's home. And every evening, except for one brief occasion, Teresa's mother refused to sit in on their discussions.

Following the second discussion, the elders gave Horacio a copy of the Book of Mormon and challenged him to begin to read and ponder its message. Within a couple of days he had devoured the contents of the book from cover to cover. As he read, he filled page after page with notes and questions, points he disagreed with or simply could not believe. The missionaries received his long lists white-faced, but determined.

"Brother Tenorio," one of them gulped, "we will answer all of your questions, but we will answer them s-l-o-w-l-y." The missionaries took Horacio's questions home to study and, over the next several evenings, thoroughly discussed each point with him, each time resolving one only to find that he had several new ones.

After many weeks of daily, diligent study and prayer, Horacio's contentious attitude began to melt away; the hope began to blossom in his soul that the gospel the missionaries were teaching him about was truly the answer he had been seeking. But he still had not received what he yearned for, a divine witness confirming its truthfulness. Then one night while he was reading the scriptures in bed, he received the answer. "The Spirit of the Lord told me 'All is true; all of what you have received from the missionaries is true,' " he explains. "I jumped out of bed with a shout and told my wife, 'I am ready to be baptized. It just came to me very clearly that this is what I must do.' "

Teresa was already converted but had not told her husband, waiting for him to reach that conclusion on his own. Horacio was not surprised to discover this sensitive spiritual capacity in his wife. "When we first met, though we were not members of the Church I knew she was very sweet, teachable, and humble," he says. "It was that, plus her strong desire to learn, progress, and find a better way of life, that drew me to her."

So on July 26, 1969, the day after their twelfth wedding anniversary, Horacio and Teresa were baptized. Six months later their daughters Maria Teresa and Monica were also baptized.

For Horacio, joining the Church was a total commitment—heart, mind, body, and soul. "We must be very obedient, very active," he told Teresa. "Now that we are members of the Church, we must do everything—study, fast, pray, pay our tithing—everything."

"Don't you feel that's a bit extreme?" she countered.

"No, I feel very good about this change in our lives. We must do it all."

The Tenorios had never attended Church meetings before—the missionaries had not taken them and they had not gone on their own—and so the Sunday after their baptism they went for the first time. When Horacio approached the bishop to pay his tithing, he was told that he had to pay in his own branch. The bishop gave him the address where that branch was located, and the next Sunday the Tenorios went in the other direction. When they found the meetinghouse, however, they were told that it wasn't their branch either.

Undaunted, the following Sunday they went to a third place and finally found where they belonged. The tiny branch, a handful of members meeting in a dilapidated apartment, was delighted to welcome the new family, which fattened the membership rolls considerably, and the Tenorios were warmly fellowshipped.

This reception reinforced them against the difficulties triggered by their joining the Church. Every aspect of their lives was affected, from their relationships with family and friends to Horacio's job and business associates.

Probably the most difficult challenge they had to deal with was the angry, hurt reaction from members of their families, who had initially seemed to accept their conversions but now wanted nothing more to do with them. Teresa's younger sister, who had been present during that first missionary discussion, had also been baptized, but soon afterwards she left the Church because of her mother's outspoken criticism. Because Horacio and Teresa were both from large, close families, rejection was painful. The emptiness this caused in their lives was filled somewhat by Church activity and their new Mormon friends, but the family schism remained. As the years have passed, family tensions have eased somewhat, and one of Horacio's brothers was eventually baptized, but all other family members continued to want nothing to do with the Church.

Soon after his baptism, Horacio began to have questions about his job and the professional ethics involved. Some people predicted he would encounter difficulty keeping the Word of Wisdom and entertaining his company's clients, but he found that not to be the case. Initially some of his long-time associates criticized his conversion and teased him about his new life-style, but as he proved his commitment to his chosen standards, they accepted the changes and their respect for him grew.

Another job-related predicament, however, was not so easily resolved. His duties as purchasing agent required negotiations with other agents, some of whom demanded unethical gifts or payments before a deal could be closed. This situation had bothered him previously, from the time he had begun working there, but now he found it intolerable. Finally he quit that job and found another one, albeit one that was less desirable, with a different company. In his new job he had to work for wages after years of being in management, but his renewed peace of mind was worth the change.

During the first year the Tenorios were members of the Church, the branch was looking for a new place to meet. The search always seemed to lead to rundown, rental properties. Finally the branch leaders decided to build a new chapel. In the completion of the building, the members of the branch made great financial sacrifices and spent endless hours in selfless labor. For Horacio and Teresa, this experience proved to be a refiner's fire, setting the pattern for years of dedicated Church service.

The Tenorios continued to mature spiritually through daily living of gospel principles, understanding of Church history, and increased familiarity with Church programs. Their progress was quickened by the demands of two decades

225

of growth for the Church in Mexico, which saw the number of stakes increase from five in 1970 to fifty-five in 1980 and ninety-six by 1990. The small branch the Tenorio family attended also grew and was divided many times until, seven years after their baptism, that same area contained five stakes comprised of thirty-five wards and branches. Such rapid growth resulted in a great need for leaders, and many, including Horacio and Teresa, responded wholeheartedly.

Immediately after joining his new branch, Horacio became a Sunday School teacher. A year later he became branch president, and when the branch was made a ward soon after, he was called to serve as bishop. Though some people expressed concern about his being bishop when he had been a member only a short time, the action was taken with the approval of the First Presidency. And in 1974, less than five years after his baptism, he became a counselor in the Mexico City North Stake. The following year Elder Howard W. Hunter of the Council of the Twelve visited the Mexico City area and created eleven new stakes, and Elder Tenorio became president of the Mexico City Mexico Satelite Stake, now the Tlalnepantla Stake.

In 1977 Horacio Tenorio was called to preside over five large regions and was also responsible for organizing a historic three-day area conference, which would be attended by President Spencer W. Kimball and several other General Authorities.

Associating with the prophet and other Brethren during the conference was the pinnacle of Elder Tenorio's spiritual experience to that time. As he met with apostles and prophets of the Lord, he reflected on a lifetime of choices and priorities that had led him to that moment. It had been a long, arduous journey since his boyhood. He was born March 6, 1935, in Mexico City, the oldest of four children born to Leopoldo Horacio and Blanca Otilia Tenorio. When he was ten, the

226

family moved to Ciudad Obregon in the Mexican state of Sonora.

Horacio's parents were well educated, Leopoldo as a chemist and Blanca as a journalist. The family lived in comfortable circumstances, with all of their physical needs provided for. Horacio grew up with a sense of independence and self-discipline, as well as with an understanding of the importance of education. Since both parents worked away from home all day, the children spent much time alone, and Horacio, as the oldest, was often responsible for cooking, cleaning, and watching the younger children. It was difficult and lonely at times, but the hours spent caring for one another fostered love and concern among the children. Leopoldo and Blanca managed to create a close, affectionate family, instilling in their children feelings of self-worth and confidence.

Then, when Horacio was twelve, his world was torn apart, for his parents got a divorce. The four children remained with their mother, and Horacio, who loved and respected his father a great deal, was bereft by his absence. He felt his father's absence most keenly during his teens, and often wished he had his support and guidance as he confronted peer pressure and difficult choices. Both parents eventually remarried – his father had six more children and his mother two – giving Horacio eight half-brothers and -sisters.

Horacio's life as a teenager bore little resemblance to his near-idyllic childhood. He missed his father, and his mother was usually at work or preoccupied with her new husband and children. Horacio, lonely and confused, turned to his friends, but it was upsetting to see them in trouble at school and with the law, stealing automobile parts and other small items. Though he longed for a sense of acceptance, he knew clearly that he did not want to become entangled in these activities, so he quit seeing his old friends and made new ones whose values and standards were more like his own.

(Eventually some of his former friends progressed to more serious crimes and served time in prison.)

Looking back, Elder Tenorio contributes his good judgment as a teenager to the example of his father, whom he describes as a moral man who wouldn't tolerate swearing or dishonesty, and to his grandfather, a constant in his life. Leopoldo Tenorio, a general in the army during the Mexican revolution, had a rigid sense of discipline and organization, but was loving and warm with his children and grandchildren. "He taught me respect for authority, for the elderly, and for my country and flag," recalls Elder Tenorio. "I can see that it is not very popular with the young people in my country today to have respect for those principles. But I am glad for his example. He was a strong pillar in my life."

Although his grandfather and grandmother, Amelia Tenorio, never joined the Church during their lives, Elder Tenorio believes they have since embraced the truth. The general and his wife came to Horacio in a dream several months after he joined the Church and, appearing anxious and worried, questioned him about the gospel. He was later reassured that their questions had been answered.

Horacio graduated from high school and studied business administration at a university in Mexico City for a year. He then continued his studies in Ciudad Obregón and eventually graduated from the Gunther Merker Institute with a post-graduate degree.

Soon after Horacio returned home from Mexico City, he noticed a vivacious young woman at a dance. He remembered having seen her years before, as he walked past her house to and from school. He had been too shy to introduce himself then, but remembered thinking, *This girl is going to be a beautiful woman.* He tucked the idea away in his mind, but now it came back to him when he was introduced to Maria Teresa de la Torre, who, at age fifteen, was indeed turning into a beautiful

228

woman. Besides her comeliness, he was attracted to her sweet nature and desire to learn. The couple dated for three years and were married on July 25, 1957, when Horacio was twenty-one and Teresa nineteen. Soon after their marriage they moved to Mexico City, believing that the city offered better opportunities for education and achievement. Both continued their education, with Teresa taking agriculture and food preparation classes. When their first daughter was born a year later, they agreed it was important that Teresa be at home full-time to care for her family, and so she did not complete her studies.

The Tenorios wanted the best possible upbringing for their children, including a firm, religious foundation. What would happen to their children in a sinful world without a definite set of standards and priorities? After they joined the Church, though the world was no less wicked, they had confidence in their daughters' ability to make good decisions.

Not long after Horacio quit his job as purchasing agent, he attended general conference in Salt Lake City in his capacity as a new bishop. When he was unable to find sacrament cups to purchase for his ward, he went to the Church's purchasing division. There he met Elder Robert E. Wells, at that time the Church's purchasing director (he later became a member of the First Quorum of the Seventy and was assigned to preside over the Mexico/Central America Area). As a result of that meeting, Bishop Tenorio was interviewed and hired as the Church's purchasing agent in Mexico. The sacrifice he had made when he chose to follow his conscience and take a less desirable job had been turned into a blessing.

One Sabbath morning Elder Tenorio, then a regional representative, was leaving his home — his family waiting in the car — when an inner voice told him, "Take your consecrated oil with you." In a hurry, he rationalized, "But I am going to church and I will not need it. Nothing is wrong." The impression came again so strongly, however, that he went back inside and retrieved the little bottle of oil.

The family attended the services and Elder Tenorio forgot about the prompting until a woman approached him in the foyer afterward and said she was looking for someone who could give a blessing. She explained that she was from the Veracruz Stake, many miles away, and had brought her three-year-old daughter to a government hospital to receive treatment for leukemia. The daughter was in a coma and the doctors had said that nothing more could be done for her. Although the woman didn't know anyone in Mexico City, she knew she must find a person with the authority to lay his hands on her daughter's head and bless her. When she saw Elder Tenorio, she knew he was the one she had been searching for. Could he please come right away? she pleaded.

"Don't worry, I can go," Bishop Tenorio assured her. Then, touching the sacred vial in his pocket, he added, "I am ready." They rushed to the child's bedside, where he blessed the gravely ill child.

Over the next few weeks Elder Tenorio called the hospital several times but was unable to get any information about the girl's condition. About six months later, the woman again came to Elder Tenorio's ward, this time to bear testimony about the experience. The day after the blessing, her daughter was completely well, she said, her voice trembling with emotion. The doctors performed tests and found no trace of the disease. Her daughter had been made whole. She also reported that other parents with children in the same hospital ward had asked her about the man in the dark suit and about the Church.

When he was called to serve as president of the Mexico Torreon Mission in 1982, Elder Tenorio had mixed emotions — joy at being called to serve, anticipation at the opportunity to work alongside his wife when most of his previous callings had caused them to spend many hours apart, but sorrow at the prospect of leaving his father, who was ill with cancer and in constant pain, with little hope of recovery. Beside his father's hospital bed, Elder Tenorio prayed that his father's pain would be eased and that, if it were his time to go, he would do so without further suffering. During their last hours together, Elder Tenorio finally had the chance to tell his father about the gospel—and his father was at last ready to listen. As they talked, the older man's heart was touched by his son's words, and he opened his soul to the gospel message. The next day he died peacefully, and two days later the Tenorios reported to the mission home in Torreon.

A few days after his arrival, President Tenorio found it necessary to make a number of changes in the missionaries' partnership assignments. Barely acquainted with the assistants and secretaries who worked in the mission home, let alone anyone else in the mission, he was faced with the difficult task of reassigning missionaries whom he knew only as pictures on a bulletin board. Over the next three days he prayerfully made the changes, seeking divine affirmation about each one. As he became acquainted with the missionaries throughout the next few months, he saw time and again that the assignments had been correct. "The Lord made the changes," he said later. "I learned how much I needed to lean on the Lord, and that if I did, he would direct my path."

Following the mission, Elder Tenorio returned to business, establishing a company to distribute irrigation systems and another company to distribute ice cream flavorings. He was also called again as a regional representative, this time over the seven stakes along Mexico's west coast.

In a country so fertile for gospel harvest, missionary work is taken seriously by everyone, from missionaries to leaders and teachers, and even new converts themselves. On one occasion Elder Tenorio attended a stake conference in the northern section of the country. When his homebound flight was canceled, he was forced to make other, less-convenient flight arrangements that required an overnight layover in La Paz, Baja California. While riding from the hotel back to the airport at six the next morning, he began a conversation with the taxi driver. "The man talked about his family with such love that I got a very good feeling about him," Elder Tenorio remembers. "I started to tell him about the gospel and he was very receptive." When they reached the airport, Elder Tenorio wrote down the man's name and address so he could send him a copy of the Book of Mormon, and he asked if he could give the man's name to the missionaries.

Soon the taxi driver and his family began learning the gospel from the missionaries, and a short time later, he and ten members of his family were baptized. "He is now a very dedicated Church leader in La Paz," adds Elder Tenorio. "It became clear to me why I had to stop that night there. I was only there for six or seven hours, but that's all the Lord needed to accomplish his work."

In March 1989 life was good for the Tenorios. Their businesses were running smoothly, and Horacio and Teresa were, as always, deeply involved in Church work. Their oldest daughter, Maria Teresa, had studied chemistry at Brigham Young University and was married with three children; Monica had also studied at BYU, and she and her small son were temporarily living with her parents; and Rocio had just returned from a mission and was completing her studies in computer science at a university in Mexico City.

Into this well-ordered routine came a message that changed everything. Their lives had been altered by a phone call before, but never so completely as this request from the First Presidency that Elder and Sister Tenorio to meet with them when they attended general conference in April. As they traveled to Salt Lake City, the Tenorios discussed possible reasons for the meeting, but they never imagined that Elder Tenorio would be called as a General Authority. At that conference he was sustained as a member of the Second Quorum of the Seventy.

Elder Tenorio's first assignment in this new calling was as first counselor to President Robert E. Wells of the Mexico/Central America Area, with Elder Carlos H. Amado, who had also just been called to the Second Quorum, as second counselor. Though Elder Tenorio's calling surprised him and his family, many persons had felt that it was only a matter of time before a Lamanite General Authority was called from Mexico. (Elder Waldo P. Call, from Colonia Juarez, Mexico, was called four years earlier, but is of European descent.)

"The blessings of having a Mexican General Authority are in harmony with the promises made to the descendants of the House of Israel—that the Lamanites shall blossom as the rose," said President Guillermo V. Torres, president of the Mexico Merida Mission and a long-time friend of Elder Tenorio. "The people in Mexico are overjoyed with his calling." He added, "Elder Tenorio is one who never looks at his clock to know when it is time to stop for the night. He is a very spiritual man with great love for the gospel; he is a great leader in the Church, as well as a great friend." (*Church News*, July 1, 1989, p. 6.)

The rapid expansion of the Church in Mexico in the 1970s and 1980s is only the beginning. It has been predicted that during the 1990s, the country will have more than thirty thousand returned missionaries, a tremendous leadership reservoir that Elder Tenorio feels will, in part, contribute to the doubling of Church membership in Mexico in that decade. As it has in the past, such growth will bring the immense challenges of fellowshipping and nurturing the progress of many new converts.

One major problem facing members of the Church in

233

Mexico, Elder Tenorio says, is economic instability. But, he adds, "poverty is a hardship that is actually a blessing for the people in Mexico and Central America. It makes us more humble. The Lord often humbles his children by sending us trials, as was the case with the earthquake in 1985. Conditions in Mexico City were becoming very bad at the time — corruption, immorality, and crime — and there were a lot of adverse feelings, a lot of tension and contention among the people. The earthquake resulted in a change in people's hearts, causing them to help and care for one another. I believe it was really a blessing. It often takes something like that to make people change their lives."

The creation of the Second Quorum of the Seventy will bless Latter-day Saints the world over, Elder Tenorio believes, but especially in Mexico, where the rapid expansion of the Church has created unique challenges. Elder Tenorio is cognizant of his role in helping to meet those challenges and of the "heavy, heavy responsibility" that comes to him as a General Authority. "I feel the Lord has opened the door to Mexico with this calling, and yet there are many, many good leaders in Mexico. I ask the Lord 'Why me?' and the only answer I can find is that I have very deep feelings inside. I am not an expert on the scriptures or genealogy, but I want to serve, and I work hard." He pauses and then adds, "and maybe this has come because I love very much the Lord."

INDEX

Abrea, Angel: is called as
General Authority, 100–101;
birth of, 101; baptism of, 102;
growth of, in Church, 104;
education of, 104; meets and
marries Maria Victoria
Chiapparino, 104–5; Church
service of, 105, 106; family of,
105, 106–7, 111; professional
career of, 105–6; political
involvement of, 107; chooses
Church service over
professional opportunity, 107;
presides over Argentina
Rosario Mission, 107–8; is
assigned as Buenos Aires
Temple president, 109;
assignments of, as General
Authority, 109, 111; expresses
philosophy of doing one's
best, 112; patterns life after
Nephi, 112–13

Abrea, Claudia Alejandra, 105,
111

Abrea, Cynthia Gabriela, 105,
106, 111

Abrea, Edealo, 101, 102–3

Abrea, Maria Victoria
Chiapparino, 100, 104–5, 110

Abrea, Oscar, 101, 104

Abrea, Patricia Viviana, 105, 111

Abrea, Zulema, 101–3, 104, 113

Amado, Andres, 214

Amado, Carlos, 207, 209–10

Amado, Carlos H.: speaks of
adversity, 204–5; testifies of
Lord's protection, 205–6;
childhood of, 207–9; baptism
of, 209–10; speaks of family's
closeness, 210; education of,
210, 212; saves money for
mission, 210–12; serves
mission in Peru, 212; meets
and marries Mayavel Pineda,
213; family and Church
service of, 213–14; presides
over Guatemala City Mission,
214; reopens El Salvador
Mission, 215; chairs
Guatemala City Temple
committee, 215–16; speaks of
sacrifice clarifying priorities,
216–17; is called as General
Authority, 217; expresses
feelings about calling, 217–18;
receives support from family,
218; serves in area presidency,
233